Campus, Brand, and Circus

A Social History of College Sports

Bassim Hamadeh, CEO and Publisher
Jennifer Codner, Senior Field Acquisitions Editor
Michelle Piehl, Project Editor
Abbey Hastings, Associate Production Editor
Miguel Macias, Senior Graphic Designer
Stephanie Kohl, Licensing Associate
Jessica Ess, Interior Designer
Natalie Piccotti, Senior Marketing Manager
Kassie Graves, Vice President of Editorial
Jamie Giganti, Director of Academic Publishing

Cover images Copyright © 2012 iStockphoto LP/gnagel.
            Copyright © 2016 iStockphoto LP/sbayram.
            Copyright © 2013 iStockphoto LP/leezsnow.
            Copyright © 2013 iStockphoto LP/RBFried.
            Copyright © 2015 iStockphoto LP/franckreporter.
            Source: https://commons.wikimedia.org/wiki/File:Claflin_University_Football_1899.jpg.

Printed in the United States of America.

ISBN: 978-1-5165-1193-8 (pbk)/978-1-5165-1194-5 (br)

Campus, Brand, and Circus

A Social History of College Sports

First Edition

Juan Javier Pescador

Michigan State University

cognella® | ACADEMIC PUBLISHING

Table of Contents

FOREWORD

Intercollegiate athletics constitute a preeminent component in the sports and entertainment industry in contemporary American society. They reflect and reproduce global trends in the production and organization of high quality entertainment for mass consumption, as well as the increasing influences of global media conglomerates on athletic competitions. They also reflect and respond to the principles and values prevalent in the social fabric and the hierarchies involving factors like race, gender, youth, and class.

College athletics have a rich and unique history in the United States and project, with their own light, some of the issues that have touched American history: racial integration, gender equity, mass entertainment, national pride, ideals of manhood and patriarchy. This textbook focuses on contemporary issues on college sports from a historical perspective and provides a panoramic overview of the metamorphosis of college athletics from their early days as recreational activities created within the bachelor culture of sporting fraternities, to present-day, twenty-four-by-seven coverage of brand revenue sports geared for mass consumption during, before, and after the academic cycles of colleges and universities in the United States.

The book introduces the reader to the major historical transformations in intercollegiate athletic competitions from their origins in nineteenth century student life to their "Big Time" status in contemporary society. It focuses on their multiple connections with youth rituals, masculine identities, gender markers, leisure cultures, racial hierarchies, and media representations.

Furthermore it analyzes the evolution of college athletics as unique forms of mass spectacle, brand marketing, regional/national identities, and global entertainment. In sum the book is designed to provide a substantial and critical introduction to the history of college sports in industrial and post-industrial American society, and its intersections with cultural representations of youth, gender, race, class, body, fitness, and power. Besides the United States, no country in the world has designed such a close connection between institutions of higher education and mass entertainment centered on physical competitions. No other country has built the largest sports infrastructure in the world to feature students as representatives of their schools, regions, and nation in athletic competitions. No other country has created the institutional category of student-athlete to classify the legal status of players or has produced coaches that earn several times over the salary of the nation's president or head of state. The transformations in college sports are vital to explain some of the most relevant features in the history of entertainment in the United States.

PREFACE

INTRODUCTION: WHY COLLEGE SPORTS HISTORY?

This chapter introduces the current debate on the social and legal status of college athletes against the historical changes of intercollegiate competitions since the mid-nineteenth century, when students in elite institutions began organizing leisure and sporting fraternities outside institutional control by school authorities. It provides a detailed analysis on the history of amateurism in college sports and the transformations operated when school authorities gained control of college sports in the early twentieth century. Moreover it presents the circumstances surrounding the student-athlete category in the 1950s and the historical and current efforts by student-athletes to have the legal status of college employees.

The chapter also provides an overview on the evolution of college sports and their social significance as youth rituals, expressions of bachelor culture and student life, and markers of masculine identities for elites in the higher education system. Finally it discusses the present-day relevance of college sports as forms of mass entertainment and their social significance as a crucial component in the sports and entertainment industry in contemporary society.

CHAPTER 1: IN THE BEGINNING

This chapter provides an overview on the genesis of intercollegiate competitions in American society between 1850 and 1870, tracing the origins of college sports in the organization of recreational and athletic activities by student associations in the country. It focuses on the emergence of college athletics as an essential element of student life, leisure fraternities and bachelor culture in nineteenth century American universities. Moreover, the chapter discusses the connections between college sports and ideals of masculinity and youth in American society, particularly the origins and development of the Muscular Christianity doctrine as a response to the challenges that urbanization and industrialization posed to the traditional ideals of patriarchy, masculinity, and youth. Finally, it discusses the role and contributions the YMCA made to the proliferation of organized sports for youth in the United States.

CHAPTER 2: AMERICAN FOOTBALL

This chapter analyzes the birth and development of football since its origins in British scholastic rugby to its ultimate metamorphosis as American football. It discusses the connections between the Yale football program and the creation of a unique sport that mirrored late nineteenth century American capitalist society, its elite values and expectations. The ideology and principles of industrial organization of time and space played a crucial role in such developments, and the leading voice in the birth of football as a capitalist metaphor for efficiency and productivity was Walter Camp, whose years at Yale led these radical transformations. The chapter also analyzes the connections between commercial capitalism, college sports, and elite institutions in higher education.

CHAPTER 3: KING FOOTBALL

This chapter focuses on the metamorphosis of college football as a form of mass entertainment in the first decades of the twentieth century, presenting the history of stadia revolution by which institutions of higher education became providers of mass spectacles in large steel-and-concrete sports facilities across the United States.

It also provides an overview of the process of institutionalization in college sports with the formation of national bodies to regulate competitions, the proliferation of athletic departments in charge of multi-sports in private and public universities, the emergence of professional coaches, and the consolidation of college athletics as a crucial element in the forging of local and regional masculine identities in American society. The chapter discusses the trajectories and contributions of legendary coaches to the sport and their consecration as father figures and national celebrities. Finally, it discusses the backlash in the 1930s against collegiate competitions for mass consumption and their multiple connections with academic life.

CHAPTER 4: THE COLD WAR AND COLLEGE SPORTS

This chapter covers the transformations of intercollegiate athletics as a response to the challenges posed by the Cold War in American society. It analyzes the ways in which college football, college/Olympic competitions, and organized sports became a high priority in government initiatives for national security. It also explores the foundation and structure of the first college sports and network television partnerships and the role of the NCAA in the reorganization of college athletics and the new status of college players as student-athletes.

CHAPTER 5: WOMEN AND COLLEGE SPORTS: AN UPHILL BATTLE

This chapter discusses the history of women in American universities and the peculiar conditions that framed their participation in physical activities and organized sports. It presents an overview of the ideological, medical, social and moral discourses that in the nineteenth century limited and constrained the full incorporation of women students in college sports. The chapter also analyzes the emergence of *modified* sports for women in the early twentieth century and the gradual advances in *no-contact* sports. It follows the struggles by female athletes to reach equal participation in sports and education after World War II and, especially, after the passing of Title IX Legislation in the 1970s. Finally, it gives a detailed analysis of the impact of Title IX on the college sports landscape in the twenty-first century.

CHAPTER 6: COLLEGE SPORTS AND AFRICAN AMERICANS

This chapter analyzes the history of African American athletes in intercollegiate athletics and their quest for inclusion and equality as athletes and students in institutions of higher education. It discusses the formal and informal means by which non-white athletes and students were excluded and discriminated against in their participation in student organizations, campus life, and college athletics, along with the ideological principles behind racial segregation in education and sports. It also analyzes the role of African American athletes in dismantling segregation in college sports after World War II and in the 1960s.

CHAPTER 7: COLLEGE SPORTS AND MASS MEDIA, 1900–1990

This chapter presents the historical transformations on how college sports have been presented, portrayed and featured by media from the late nineteenth century to the satellite/digital communication era. It provides an overview on the main venues to disseminate information about intercollegiate athletics, from student newspapers to the commercial radio broadcasting days, the arrival of network television, and the changes implemented in the 1990s with the proliferation of cable television and digital broadcasting. It provides a detailed analysis of how colleges have interacted with mass media corporations and how college sports have led the country in sports broadcasting, from "single package" telecasting contracts to the formation of media outlets to cover college athletics exclusively on cable and digital outlets.

CHAPTER 8: BIG TIME COLLEGE SPORTS: U-BRAND REVENUE-SPORTS

This chapter analyzes the consolidation of Big Time college sports, namely football and basketball as national brands in sports entertainment, closely linked to mass media conglomerates and the global entertainment industry. It presents an overview of the multiple connections between college revenue sports, mass entertainment and mass consumerism. Moreover the chapter emphasizes the intersections between college sports and pubic opinion, the increasing voices for reform as well as the challenges intercollegiate athletics face in the twenty-first century.

INTRODUCTION

Why College Sports History?

A merican intercollegiate athletics represent a unique feature in the
history of sports in modern times and a quintessential element in the
history of entertainment and spectacles for mass consumption. Despite
their elitist and high-class origins in private and exclusive institutions
in the Northeast, college sports have been a central component of the
American way of life throughout the twentieth century. Seen as an example of American exceptionalism during the Cold War or the consummate
model of for-the-love-of-the-game sports since the early 1900s, college
sports have developed a unique relationship with mass media that cannot
be identified with other types of organized sports. Print media, newspapers, magazines, radio broadcasting, network television, and later, digital
media, have relied on college sports as a primary form of entertainment
nationwide. College sports have been at the forefront in each mass media
revolution in American history. Printed media in the nineteenth century,
radio broadcasting in the 1920s, network television in the 1950s, cable in
the 1970s, and digital media in contemporary society have all featured
college sports on a regular basis.

The sports infrastructure created by intercollegiate athletics has no
equivalent in the United States or in the world. The top ten largest stadiums in the country were built for college sports, with eighteen college
sports stadiums ranked in the top twenty. The National Football League
(NFL) only has two stadiums in the top twenty; Major League Baseball
(MLB) has none.

A common misperception is that college sports are not organized in
an efficient and professional fashion. However, intercollegiate athletics
was the first to negotiate broadcasting rights with radio. Similarly, the
National Collegiate Athletic Association (NCAA) led the way in negotiating television broadcasting rights in a single package in the 1950s. In
similar developments, college sports were the top sports events covered
by cable and digital media. The history of college sports is also the history of innovation, progress, and consolidation of sports as a form of

entertainment for mass consumption in the United States. More recently, the complex and multilayered interactions between college sports and mass media give insight into the symbiotic metamorphoses of professional sports as media conglomerates.

College sports also led the country in implementing nutritional, dietary, physical, and psychological principles to maximize performance on the field. Likewise, intercollegiate athletics were the first to incorporate scientific and technological advances to gain a competitive advantage against opposing teams, revolutionizing not only intercollegiate competitions but also professional sports altogether.

College sports, moreover, have a long trajectory in successfully crafting and displaying a unique legal status in state and federal courts. The several interactions between the NCAA and the US Supreme Court represent a clear example of the ways in which organizations and corporations have successfully carved out exemptions and privileges in the national legal system.

The images produced by intercollegiate athletics throughout the twentieth century have also been central to the construction and display of notions and ideals on masculinity, femininity, youth, beauty, and national identity. Moreover, college sports have reflected and reproduced hierarchies of race, gender, and class across history.

College sports history is a unique space to analyze the various ways in which women have been segregated and discriminated against at the highest official levels in institutions of higher education. As athletes, as well as students, American women have a unique historical experience in overcoming institutional barriers and challenges in the field for gender equality in the classroom and in the sports arena. While the struggles of female athletes mirrored the battles of women in general, their experiences with discrimination in college sports have not been fully recognized by sports historians nor analyzed in sports history classes.

College athletics have also been a unique social space where racial hierarchies are reflected, re-created, enforced, challenged, and modified. While not exempted from their own racial stratification and connections with Jim Crow laws, college sports have traditionally been at the forefront in the struggle for desegregation and equality along ethnic and racial lines. Racial integration in intercollegiate athletics predates similar developments in the MLB, the NFL, and other professional sports.

Amateurs, Student-Athletes, and Scholarship Players

College athletics have been essential to university life since the 1850s in the Northeastern Seaboard and in the aftermath of the Civil War nationwide.

Students have participated as athletes representing their institutions in many competitions for over 150 years in American history. The involvement of students as sports figures has undergone multiple metamorphoses and cannot be reduced to simple opposites (amateur/professional, clean/corrupt, student/ringer, student/employee, and so on). Institutional and legal definitions regarding the status of college athletes have changed and evolved since the beginnings of organized intercollegiate sports. For instance, the student-athlete formula adopted by the NCAA in the 1950s assured the existence of monetary compensation, services, and benefits for college athletes, yet prevented them from claiming compensation as employees in case of severe injuries resulting from their participation in a given sport.

The legal and institutional status of athletes has been a constant source of contention and struggle between university officials, players, students, and alumni. It is a common misconception that college players have been trying to gain workers' rights if not employee status only in recent times. While the legal status of college athletes as student-athletes and not university workers has not experienced significant transformations since 1953, college players have engaged in legal actions trying to secure compensation and benefits in several instances before and after the formal recognition of their particular legal categorization. Athletes have had a long history of participating in struggles to secure benefits as individuals and groups.

Jocks: Myth and History

According to popular culture, college athletes are supposed to be unintelligent, primitive, homophobic, rude, arrogant, self-centered, misogynistic, aggressive, and prone to crime, violence, alcohol, sex, and drugs. In general, they are portrayed in a distorted/perverted view and seen as examples of everything that is wrong with mass sports organized by institutions of higher education.[1]

Media entertainment in cinema, network television, and other venues has traditionally portrayed college athletes as antagonists, while media news highlights their illegal and immoral activities on a regular basis. The history of college athletes, however, provides a much more complex and different landscape.

In the nineteenth century, student communities played a pivotal role in organizing intercollegiate sports. Fraternities, clubs, associations, and committees took charge of intramural and intercollegiate competitions according to their own traditions, rituals, and rules. The first generations of college athletes, from 1850s crew squads to 1880s football teams, usually came from the same socioeconomic, ideological, and political background as the rest of the other students. As college sports became a venue to stratify and create social hierarchies within the student body and in relation to students in other institutions, athletes represented the best and brightest in each class. In the last decades of the twentieth century, however, the drive for success and the expansion of college athletics into various sports with a full competition calendar created the need for more talented, specialized, and efficient types of athletes. Student organizations commonly resorted to luring people to their campus on the basis of athletic skills and potential sports contributions to bolster the reputation of the alma mater institution. Using hired hands, individuals who had played professional baseball, ringers who had participated as athletes for other universities, and so on became commonly used resources to elevate the competitive qualities of specific squads and sports. It was not uncommon to witness these nontraditional students as prominent athletes in rowing competitions, baseball matches, and football contests.

In 1906 the recently formed Intercollegiate Athletics Association (IAA) took a firm step in attempting to get rid of the use of rogue players and establish the foundations for policies that fully protected the amateur status of student players. According to the IAA's bylaws:

> No student shall represent a College or University in an intercollegiate game or contest who is paid or receives, directly or indirectly, any money or financial concession or emolument as past or present compensation for, or as prior consideration or inducement to play in, or enter any athletic contest, whether the said remuneration be received from, or paid by, or at the instance of any organization, committee or faculty of such College or University, or any individual whatever.[2]

The first definition of amateurs by the IAA strictly prohibited any type of compensation in currency, benefits, or services for college students representing their institution in intercollegiate sports. The association also banned any form of recruitment, making clear that the student and future athlete should always come to the university and never the opposite. Despite the IAA's strong rules for amateurism, in reality all big programs nationwide recruited students from high schools and preparatory schools.

Coaches also resorted to the practice of raiding, or recruiting students already playing for other colleges. Using many sorts of inducements, from cash to ghost jobs and other perks, coaches consistently looked for talented players to transfer to their institution and play ball for them. Since the IAA was defined basically as a national rules committee for football (and later for other college sports), the responsibilities for the enforcement of rules on the amateur status of athletes always rested on the individual programs and, in some cases, their conferences. This situation opened the door for continuous abuses by coaches and programs.

In 1916, the IAA officially became the National Collegiate Athletic Association, or NCAA. The redefined organism was in charge of standardizing football rules and regulating other college sports competitions. In this context the national organization provided a new institutional definition for college players and their amateur status. The 1916 association's new rule stated that an amateur was one

> who participates in competitive physical sports only for pleasure, and the physical, mental, moral, and social benefits directly derived therefrom.[3]

A slightly different concept was implemented in the NCAA rules in 1922, by which an amateur athlete in college sports was defined as

> one who engages in sport solely for the physical, mental or social benefits he derives therefrom, and to whom the sport is nothing more than an avocation.[4]

Despite having the amateur status of athletes defined as one of the essential targets in the NCAA's general mission, during the 1920s and 1930s coaches and athletic departments in competitive programs continued to use illegal methods, which took advantage of the fact that the enforcement of amateur rules remained in the hands of each institution. In Big Ten and other conferences, rival teams would usually challenge the status of one of the key players on the opposite team. These challenges would be presented in the media, where the accusing party would be in charge of stating evidence to support its claim. The accused program would deny the charges, counter with a similar accusation, or simply state that there was no evidence to keep the player in question on the sidelines. Only sporadically would football programs be liable for fielding players with questionable amateur credentials. In the worst-case scenario the accused player would be benched for the game against the plaintiff institution.

Sanity Code of 1948

The NCAA did not perceive the notion of athletic scholarships in very favorable terms, since it basically represented a radical departure from the standards of amateurism and the definition of college sports as an avocation. As the football seasons became normalized in the aftermath of World War II, the leadership of the organization decided to terminate the practice and adopt a uniform policy for the regulation of institutional financial aid for college athletes. The new regulations, known as the Sanity Code, established a firm prohibition of scholarships granted to student players on the basis of their athletic skills. No more athletic scholarships would be tolerated. In addition, the new rules allowed athletes to receive institutional financial help and scholarships based on academic merit or economic need. This formal establishment of financial aid for athletes represented a radical departure from the first NCAA amateur regulations (1906–1947). College players were nominally entitled to the same type of financial support as the general student population, while athletic scholarships were condemned to extinction. NCAA regulations made clear that such grants could not be tied to any form of athletic performance and that, once granted, such scholarships could not be revoked for nonacademic reasons.

College Players and the History of Their Legal Status

Ernest Nemeth played for the University of Denver. In 1950, he sustained a severe back injury during football practice. Nemeth and several other players had jobs in the university in maintenance services at the stadium, field house, and other sports facilities. Nemeth sued the institution for compensation, arguing that he was employed by the university to play football and that the injury he suffered arose from his fulfillment of labor duties. The court favored the plaintiff, and the University of Denver filed an appeal, arguing that Nemeth's employment duties were limited to keeping the tennis courts free from gravel and that this job was completely unconnected to Nemeth's football activities. The Colorado court rejected the argument and established the following:

> It appears from the record that Nemeth was informed by those having authority at the University, that "it would be decided on the football field who receives the meals and the jobs." He participated in football practice, and after a couple of weeks a list of names was read, which list included Nemeth's name, and he was then given free meals and a job. One witness said: "If you worked hard (in football) you got a meal ticket." Another testified that, "the man who produced in football would get the meals and a job." The football coach testified that meals and the job ceased when the student was "cut from the football squad."[5]

The 1953 ruling in Colorado set a major precedent in the potential status of college players, since the ruling established that the Workmen's Compensation Act could be applied to athletes injured while representing a college institution. According to the opinion of the Colorado Supreme Court:

> In the instant case the employment at the University, so far as Nemeth was concerned, was dependent on his playing football, and

he could not retain his job without playing football. The evidence before the Industrial Commission was to the effect that his job and other remuneration incident thereto came to an end when he ceased to "make good" in football. Under the record as here made, the Commission and the District Court may have properly concluded as they did determine that Nemeth was an employee of the University and sustained an accidental injury arising out of and in the course of his employment.[6]

The NCAA strongly reacted to the notion of athletes as university employees and its potential ramifications in the labor and legal arenas. NCAA executive director Walter Byers argued the organization's position by explaining the origins of the student-athlete concept:

> It was then that they [colleges] came face to face with a serious, external threat that prompted most of the colleges to unite and insist, with one voice, that, grant-in-aid or not, college sports were only for "amateurs."
>
> That threat was the dreaded notion that NCAA athletes could be identified as employees by state industrial commissions and the courts.
>
> We crafted the term student-athlete, and soon it was embedded in all NCAA rules and interpretations as a mandated substitute for such words as players and athletes. We told college publicists to speak of "college teams," not football or basketball "clubs," a common word to the pros.
>
> I suppose none of us wanted to accept what was really happening. That was apparent in the behind-the-scenes agonizing over the issue of workmen's compensation for players.[7]

After Nemeth's claim against the University of Denver, another prominent case developed in California. Edward Gary Van Horn enrolled at California State Polytechnic in 1956, and he was invited to play for the institution's football team. Van Horn worked in the college cafeteria and earned money from various other sources, including a scholarship from the institution. One of his jobs was working for the athletic department lining the field. The funds for the athletic scholarship came from the Mustang Booster Club, which granted similar scholarships to potential athletes based on the coach's recommendations.

On October 28, 1960, the Mustangs played Bowling Green. After the match, the team left on a plane from Toledo, Ohio. Unfortunately, soon after take-off the plane crashed, killing twenty-two passengers, sixteen of them football players. Van Horn's widow, Kate Van Horn, sued California State Polytechnic for death benefits on behalf of her minor children and herself. The courts rejected the claim on the basis that Van Horn was on a scholarship. According to the case records:

> Petitioners' contention is that decedent participated in the college football program under a contract of employment with the college. Respondents contend that decedent's participation in football was voluntary and the "scholarship" was a gift, not payment for services. The commission, after reconsideration, affirmed the referee's denial of benefits to petitioners and adopted his conclusions that decedent was not an employee of the college, there was no contract of employment or hire, and, in any event, playing on the college football team was not "rendering services" within the meaning of the Workmen's Compensation Act.[8]

The court stated in its conclusion against Kate Van Horn:

> The opinion of the commission sets forth the proposition that to conclude that one who has an athletic scholarship is an employee entitled to workmen's compensation benefits would impose a heavy burden on institutions of learning, would discourage the granting of scholarships, and, therefore, would be against public policy. We find no authority to the effect that an award in the present instance would be against public policy. ... It cannot be said as a matter of law that every student who receives an "athletic scholarship" and plays on the school athletic team is an employee of the school. To so hold would be to thrust upon every student who so participates an employee status to which he has never consented and which would deprive him of the valuable right to sue for damages. Only where the evidence establishes a contract of employment is such inference reasonably to be drawn. State Comp. Ins. Fund v. Industrial Com., 135 Colo. 570 [314 P.2d 288], cited by respondents, is a case in which a member of a college football team received a scholarship for tuition. There the evidence did not establish a contract of hire to play football and thus did not support a finding of an employee-employer relationship.[9]

The appeal court ruled in favor of Van Horn's widow, raising new concerns in the NCAA leadership with regard to the potential application of the Workmen's Compensation Act for college athletes.

In 1973, the NCAA Convention adopted a change in the legal framework regarding financial aid and athletics. Proposal 39 stipulated that grant-in-aid scholarships should not be assigned in multiyear packages but instead should only cover a maximum period of one year, with the possibility of renewal according to the standards of each institution. The change from the four-year to year-by-year format allowed institutions to closely monitor the performance of student-athletes and use the renewal clause to expand control over them.

Figure I.1   Kain Colter Press Conference, Chicago, Illinois, 2014.

In 2014, the National Labor Relations Board (NLRB) received a petition by football players of Northwestern University who received athletic scholarships to be classified as employees and thereby initiate the process of being represented for the purposes of collective bargaining. In the summary of the facts, the NLRB established that 85 out of 115 players received athletic or grant-in-aid scholarships that covered tuition, fees, room, board, and book expenses, a total of $61,000 per player a year. Through the four-year scholarship offer or tender, the players understood that the grant-in-aid could be reduced or canceled according to conditions and circumstances not applicable to other students at the institution. Such subjection of the scholarship football players to special rules included detailed norms about private behavior:

> Players are required to disclose to their coaches detailed information pertaining to the vehicle they drive. The players must also abide by a social media policy, which restricts what they can post in the internet, including Twitter, Facebook and Instagram. In fact the players are prohibited from denying a coach's "friend" request and the former's posts are monitored. ... Players are prohibited from profiting of their image or reputation, including the selling of merchandise and autographs. Players are also required to sign a release permitting the Employer and the Big

> Ten Conference to utilize their name, likeness and image for any purpose. The players are subject to strict drug and alcohol policies ... anti-hazing and anti-gambling policies as well.[10]

The NLRB established that during football season (August to November), players were required to devote fifty to sixty hours a week to football and football-related activities, and that if the team made it to a bowl game, an additional forty to fifty hours per week would be added in the month of December. During winter and spring football seasons, players were also required to participate in football-related activities twelve to fifteen hours per week and twenty to twenty-five hours per week respectively.

According to the NLRB's findings, scholarship players were identified and recruited primarily because of their football abilities and potential contribution to the program. The revenue generated by Northwestern University football in the NCAA Football Bowl Subdivision passed the $31 million mark for the 2012–2013 season and reached $235 million for the period between 2003 and 2013, from ticket sales, television broadcasting rights, merchandise sales, and licensing rights.

After evaluating the applicable legal standard for the common law definition of *employee*, the NLRB established the following:

> 1. Grant-in-Aid Scholarship Football Players Perform Services for the Benefit of the Employer for Which They Receive Compensation. ...
>
> 2. Grant-in-Aid Scholarship Football Players are Subject to the Employer's Control in the Performance of Their Duties as Football Players. ...
>
> 3. The Employer's Grant-in-Aid Scholarship Players are Employees Under the Common Law Definition.[11]

The NLRB ruled that the scholarship players were not primarily students:

> The players spend 50 to 60 hours per week on their football duties during a one-month training camp prior to the start of the academic year and an additional 40 to 50 hours per week on those duties during the three or four month football season. Not only is this more hours than many undisputed full-time employees work at their jobs, it is also many more hours than the players spend on their studies. In fact, the players do not attend academic classes while in training camp or for the first few weeks of the regular season. After the academic year begins, the players still continue to devote 40 to 50 hours per week on football-related activities while only spending about 20 hours per week attending classes. Obviously, the players are also required to spend time studying

and completing their homework as they have to spend time practicing their football skills even without the direct orders of their coaches. But it cannot be said that they are "primarily students" who "spend only a limited number of hours performing the athletic duties."[12]

The NLRB rejected the notion that scholarship players were engaging in athletic activities as a way to advance toward the completion of their educational degree requirements, establishing that they were not supervised or trained by faculty and that their athletic responsibilities had no connection to the core elements of their college degrees. Moreover, the NLRB denied the alternate claims that scholarship players were temporary employees or that they received financial aid but not compensation. Finally, the NLRB ruled that scholarship players could initiate efforts toward labor organization.

While the success of the Northwestern players' petition made a significant impact on the national media, the university followed through with an appeal to the NLRB in Washington, DC, the following year. The review produced a different outcome. In the summer of 2015, the NLRB declined to assert jurisdiction on the petition by Northwestern football players to be considered university employees. Since fewer than 20 institutions out of the 125 that made up the Football Bowl Subdivision are private, the NLRB decided that asserting jurisdiction would not contribute to the stability of Division I football programs, most of which are in the hands of public universities. Having no authority to rule on the status of public employees, the NLRB decided not to rule on the petition of the Northwestern players, since Northwestern University is the only private school in the Big Ten Conference. The NLRB did not rule, however, against the petition or against the status of the players as university workers. That, of course, only left the door open for the next wave of court disputes regarding the legal status of college athletes.

No less important in the decision was the change in the terminology applied to college players by the NLRB. The student-athlete category is nowhere to be found in the document. While declining to rule whether college athletes are employees or students, the NLRB referred to them as "scholarship players" and established that they provide services in exchange for compensation by their institutions. The scholarship player definition represents a pivotal point in the legal status of college athletes, for it implies a recognition of the contractual obligations between players and schools, tacitly recognizes that the relationship involves an exchange of athletic services and economic compensation, and finally, obliterates the word *student* as an identity term and defining element for intercollegiate athletics.

The new definition of scholarship players, according to the NLRB, states that

> scholarship players do not fit into any analytical framework that the Board has used in cases involving other types of students or athletes. In this regard the scholarship players bear little resemblance to the graduate student assistants or student janitors and cafeteria workers whose employee status the Board has considered in other cases. The fact that the scholarship players are students who are also athletes receiving a scholarship to participate in what has traditionally been regarded as an extracurricular activity (albeit a nationally prominent and extraordinarily lucrative one for many universities, conferences and the NCAA) materially sets them apart from the Board's student precedent. Yet at the same time, the scholarship players are unlike athletes in undisputedly professional leagues, given that the scholarship players are required, inter alia, to be enrolled full time as students and meet various academic requirements, and they are prohibited by NCAA regulations from engaging in many of the types of activities that professional athletes are free to engage in, such as profiting from the use of their names and likenesses.[13]

The NLRB also established several similarities between the NCAA Football Bowl Subdivision and professional sports, while establishing that ruling for one specific football program (Northwestern) would alter the stability of the labor relations prevalent in the NCAA and conferences *league-wide.* The NLRB has ruled on similar bargaining processes for the NFL (1973 and 1992) and other professional sports, but those rulings applied to the entire leagues. Since 85 percent of the programs at the Football Bowl Subdivision belong to public universities, the NLRB stated that

> asserting jurisdiction would not have that effect because the Board cannot regulate most FBS programs. Accordingly, asserting jurisdiction would not promote stability in labor relations.[14]

Between 1906 and 2016, the institutional and legal status of college players underwent significant metamorphoses. While financial aid and any type of monetary compensation were explicitly prohibited by schools, conferences, and national organizations, the arrival of athletic scholarships in the 1930s and the 1948 NCAA approval of economic and/or academic scholarships redefined the amateur status of college athletes in profound and irreversible ways. The official implementation of a new policy in 1956 by which athletic or grant-in-aid scholarships could sponsor most football players and other athletes symbolized the national institutionalization of economic compensation in exchange for athletic services by college students. While various legal disputes in the 1950s and 1960s to secure injury compensation rights for athletes produced mixed results for the petitioners, the trend to classify players as workers or employees has gained significant momentum as *revenue college sports* are featured prominently in the national media and through digital multiplatform standards. The Northwestern football players' initiative is just the most recent development in the continuous search to define the legal status and social place for college athletes and college athletics. While it is impossible to predict the outcome of this contested issue, it is fairly obvious that the struggle is far from over.

Virility and College Sports

Charles Caldwell, legendary Princeton University coach, presented football as follows in his *Modern Football for the Spectator*:

> When football is kept in its proper perspective it can be of great value to players and spectators alike. ... The many ramifications of the sport are invaluable in the development of young men of many qualities that are needed for adult citizenship and leadership. The obvious ones of physical strength, courage and stamina are only part of the story. Even more important are the elements of discipline, team play, self less cooperation, and loyalty. The ability to think under the double pressures of physical contact and psychological urgency is of paramount importance. ... The understanding and appreciation of the organization of modern football, its strategy, can provide very real training from fitting young men into similar problems of organization and execution in business, professional and military pursuits.[5]

Caldwell's perspective, linking college sports to a liminal gate through which young males become successful adults, belongs to a long tradition in American history that links supervised physical activities and organized sports to the best way to turn boys into men, students into leaders, and individuals into citizens. College sports have been defined, and to a large extent are still seen, as man-making social spaces. Likewise, coaches, trainers, athletic directors, and school officials have consistently established an image as youth guardians and authorities on the masculine metamorphosis of American boys into complete adults.

Since its origins in the late nineteenth century, organized intercollegiate athletics have been connected to American values and masculine prowess. According to Ronald A. Smith, a prominent historian of college sports:

> [In 1897] A University of Georgia football player, Richard Von Gammon, was killed in a game against the University of Virginia. Soon the Georgia legislature passed a bill prohibiting football. Yet, when the mother of

the victim deplored the ban and Georgia's governor vetoed the bill, they were reflecting a late-nineteenth century value stronger than the belief that football was violent. The value was expressed through a belief in the importance of developing virile, manly virtues from the vigorous game of football. ... Football became symbolic of not only the manliness of colleges but also of American life.[16]

Sports have traditionally been a landscape to display masculinity, a social space to showcase the brightest and best of manly attributes: courage, discipline, sacrifice, loyalty, perseverance, and hope. Originally attached to religious rituals and harvest festivities, preindustrial sports consistently functioned as performances of manhood, where men were separated from boys, and boys were separated from girls. Patriarchal societies featured sports to perform and enhance the differences between those who could assume paterfamilias roles as protectors, producers, and providers and those who could not, by virtue of their age, gender, or physical condition.

The industrialization and urbanization of the United States created the conditions to catapult sports and other recreational activities as a social *manscape* where masculinity was represented and re-created.[17]

College athletics enjoys a unique place among all spaces in which masculinity is re-created and reasserted, since it includes youth, power, and success as core elements of the competition. On the one hand, universities have been guardians of youth and shapers of the future paterfamilias and citizens. On the other hand, alumni, school authorities, and to some extent, the public at large have identified intercollegiate athletics as a central representation of their own youth and their own generational upbringing. Institutions of higher education throughout the twentieth century have not only assumed the role of "man-makers," they have also become a powerful symbol of the masculine features of previous generations reenacted by sports for mass entertainment.

Institutional Masculinity and Manly Theater

In the nineteenth century the traditional roles of masculinity deteriorated in American society as a result of large processes of urbanization and industrialization. The heroic artisan as manly model was diminished in its social relevance as large numbers of men moved into cities to work in environments of mass production, where the individual and personal features had significantly less importance.

Moreover, the conditions for social control in urban areas represented a challenge for religious and civic authorities. Whereas local priests and town authorities had had a consistent hegemony in rural areas over the families and communities, in nineteenth-century American society the patriarchal structures had to be realigned to adapt to the new circumstances brought into place by the industrialization of the country. City life made patriarchal control less effective, especially with respect to the control of leisure activities and free time. While attending church on Sundays was close to being a universal ritual in rural communities, life in the cities presented a new challenge to religious authorities. Likewise, parental control in urban areas, densely populated by young adults and teenagers recently arrived from the countryside or countries in Europe, faced significant challenges. The single population had far more opportunities in the cities to socialize beyond the limits of parental control. In many cases fathers and mothers were not even physically present to exert authority in the household, as the immigration and migration waves into American cities involved mainly young generations. It is therefore not by chance that patriarchal leaders had a consistently grim perspective of youth in urban and industrial areas.

For most of the twentieth century, the college campus was established and considered a gendered social landscape, where male behavior and power were to be nurtured, reenacted, displayed, and re-created as public spectacle. American universities in the industrial era have exercised substantial control over the social spaces where students live and learn, from dorms, classrooms, and cafeterias to social groups, extracurricular activities, and moral standards. Campuses across the United States are not only learning environments, but also imagined communities regulated by the school's unique set of rules involving health, moral, and ideological issues.

Like other institutions with similar authority (army, navy, penitentiary system, and so on) universities exert considerable control over the student population in their academic and nonacademic activities, and their social behavior and lifestyle in general. As a surrogate paterfamilias, the American university has established heterosexual, white male hegemonic values as the general model of the institutional standards for all students. American white manhood has consistently been a core principle of university life in the twentieth and twenty-first centuries. Under such ideological principles, organized athletics and intercollegiate competitions facilitate the bonding between returning and new students, between students and authorities, and between students and the institution. College competitions for mass entertainment feature an almost exclusively male spectacle that re-creates masculine hegemonic values as endorsed by university tradition and culture.

> The Harvard-educated Senator Henry Cabot Lodge spoke for the manly game of football at Harvard commencement festivities. "The time given to athletic contests and the injuries incurred on the playing field," he

stated in an address to the Harvard class of 1896, "are part of the price which the English-speaking race has paid for being world-conquerors."[18]

STUDY QUESTIONS

1. Discuss the evolutionary changes in the status of amateurism between 1900 and 1930.

2. Discuss the stereotypes of college athletes in popular culture.

3. Discuss the legal disputes between college players and their institutions regarding injury compensation.

4. Define the motivation to classify college players as student athletes in the 1950s.

5. Discuss the arguments to identify college players as employees.

6. Discuss the relevance of the 2014–2015 legal petition by Northwestern football players.

7. Define the elements of traditional masculinity in the preindustrial United States.

8. Identify the ways in which higher education has been connected to youth and masculine adulthood.

9. Discuss how masculinity is re-created and celebrated in public collegiate competitions.

10. Discuss the role of coaches as father figures in college sports.

ADDITIONAL READING

Byers, Walter. *Unsportsmanlike Conduct: Exploiting College Athletes*. With Chris Hammer. Ann Arbor: University of Michigan Press, 2010.

Fram, Nicholas, and T. Ward Frampton. "A Union of Amateurs: A Legal Blueprint to Reshape Big-Time College Athletics." *Buffalo Law Review* 60 (2012): 1003–77.

Kimmel, Michael. *Manhood in America: A Cultural History*. New York: Free Press, 1996.

Kimmel, Michael. *Misframing Men: The Politics of Contemporary Masculinity*. New Brunswick, NJ: Rutgers University Press, 2010.

McCormick, Robert A., and Amy C. McCormick, "The Myth of the Student-Athlete: The College Athlete as Employee." *Washington Law Review* 81, no. 71 (2006): 95–157.

Muenzen, Kristen R. "Weakening Its Own Defense? The NCAA's Version of Amateurism." *Marquette Law Sports Review* 13, no. 2 (Spring 2003): 257–88. http://scholarship.law .marquette.edu/cgi/viewcontent.cgi?article=1276&context=sportslaw.

Porto, Brian L. *The Supreme Court and the NCAA: The Case for Less Commercialism and More Due Process in College Sports*. Ann Arbor: University of Michigan Press, 2012.

US NLRB Northwestern University and College Athlete Players Association (CAPA), Petitioner. Case 13-RC-121359. Chicago, IL. March 26, 2014.

US NLRB Northwestern University and College Athlete Players Association (CAPA), Petitioner. Case 13-RC-121359. Washington, DC, August 17, 2015.

FIGURE CREDIT

Figure I.1: Antonio Perez, "Kain Colter press conference, Chicago Illinois, 2014." Copyright © 2014 by Newscom. Reprinted with permission.

1

In the Beginning

Organized sports featuring students as competitors in athletic events are a rather late development in the history of American colleges and universities. Following the foundation of Harvard University in the seventeenth century (1636), the first wave of universities in the colonies did not pass the ten mark. The College of William & Mary (1693), Yale University (1701), the University of Pennsylvania (1740), King's College (1754; later renamed Columbia University), and the College of Charleston (1770), among others, were founded as predominantly religious institutions with the mission of educating the next generation of ministers in specific denominational groups. None of these institutions had any interest in organizing athletics competitions of any sort. Sports were considered a distraction from student work and a distraction from God and consequently enjoyed no respect from university officials, most of whom were leading members of specific religious denominations.[19]

The American Revolution (1776–1783) and the first decades of independence did not alter this structure. For decades, and centuries for a few of these institutions, college authorities showed no interest in organizing or regulating any physical activities for the student body. Historians have yet to identify any record of intercollegiate competitions prior to the nineteenth century.

Student athletic activities emerged in connection with the very active student life outside the limits of official supervision in the early and mid-nineteenth century. These athletic activities were organized by and for student groups and formed part of wider youth rituals, through which students created a leisure lifestyle while attending the educational institution. Nineteenth-century student life included various happenings organized at different levels: dining clubs, reading societies, fraternities, outing clubs, secret societies, political associations, and so on. From such a vibrant extracurricular student life, American universities witnessed the emergence of college sports.

Historical records at Princeton University indicate the existence of regular games and contests run by undergraduates since the 1760s.[20] Similar findings from Harvard have also established a pulsating development of games with sticks, balls, and footballs. Incoming students would participate in athletic games as part of their ritual initiation and subordination to the upper classes. Kicking a football on a common, running, and displaying athletic skills and strengths were intrinsic to student life at such institutions.

Football games between different classes became a strong tradition by the 1820s at both Harvard and Princeton, followed by other institutions in the Northeast. *Rounders, town ball*, and other ancestors of *baseball* were also regular features in student activities. The organization, rules, and supervision of these games were completely in the hands of upper-class undergraduates, who followed traditions established by previous generations. Since each college followed its own traditions, games were not standardized, nor did they have a government body in charge of laying out a general set of rules.[21]

From the origins of higher education in the United States, sports were developed as a pastime for undergraduates with little or no attention from school officials. The only way in which school authorities would participate in these events was in trying to curb them to limit violence and potentially disruptive behavior.

Leisure Life on Campus

American universities are substantially different from their European and Latin American counterparts in three important aspects. First, while European universities are mainly located in metropolitan areas, most American colleges have been deliberately founded in small and isolated communities in order to avoid urban distractions for the student body, provide an ideal environment for learning, and facilitate the control of the student population. Second, American universities created with public funding have been the responsibility and duty of states and not the federal government. Since the nineteenth century, public universities have been founded by state legislatures with land and resources coming from each state. State sovereign authority on the public university extends from assigning its physical location to providing an annual budget. In fact, the appointment of the location of a state university has been almost as relevant as that of a state capital. The establishment of state universities in the United States have been some of the first legal actions made by several state governments. For example, Michigan's first university was created in Detroit in 1817, and re-founded in

Ann Arbor in the 1830s. Lastly, American universities, following the example of the Harvard University campus, have generated the college town or college campus town—a unique urban and social space where students, workers, and residents interact on a regular basis. The college town social life has no similar development in other universities around the globe. While non-American students attend classes and participate in extracurricular activities, they mingle with the urban population in terms of housing and leisure. American students in college towns take classes together, live together, and participate in non-academic activities as members of a student group. Therefore, socialization in American colleges is a unique process.

In the early nineteenth century, an intense student life on campus generated the formation of sports clubs, traditional games, and interclass contests as regular features of undergraduate leisure. Football, cricket, town ball, running, walking, and rowing were among the most popular athletic pastime activities, laid out according to the traditional ways of each institution.[22]

The college fraternity started at William and Mary in 1776 and became a popular option for students in the 1820s and an important venue to access many student-run activities, from literary debates to dining societies and secret organizations. In the 1840s the Greek system proliferated outside Northeastern private institutions and set permanent roots in public and private universities in other areas nationwide. Greek societies shaped student life across campuses in the nation and brought together alumni and students.

After the Civil War, the largest fraternities had between twenty-five and fifty chapters nationwide with alumni as prominent members including judges, ministers, politicians, financiers, and military men. Fraternities played a pivotal role in the organization of student life, leisure activities, and organized sports. By 1879 there were more than sixty active student fraternities with over 60,000 members and seventy alumni chapters.[23]

British colleges and schools started the first intercollegiate athletic competitions in the early nineteenth century. Students from Eton, Harrow, Oxford, and Cambridge took the traditional intramural competitions to the next level in the 1820s, particularly with the sports of rugby and crew.[24] Within a few years, Northeastern American undergraduates would follow these trends to create the first intercollegiate competitions in the United States.

Crew

Yale undergraduates formed a boat club in 1843, a development that would generate the first official cross-college athletic competition in the country. Following the example of the Oxford-Cambridge rivalry, a rowing race between Harvard and Yale was agreed on in 1852: a two-mile course on Lake

Winnipesaukee, New Hampshire. Rowing was therefore the first college sport organized in the United States. In the 1850s Yale established the lead with twelve intramural boating clubs and a sophisticated competition system to produce the best possible athletes to play against other schools.[25]

Rowing in rivers and harbors across the Northeastern communities in the United States had been a consistent tradition since colonial times, and in the 1820s the Hudson River hosted competitions between British and American crews. Upper classes in urban areas considered rowing a healthy recreational activity in which they performed in public and displayed their social status as leaders. Regatta contests brought together wealthy crews and lower-class spectators, rivaling other outdoor social events. Amateur rowing clubs proliferated and became favored choices for recreational activities for those who could afford the expenses of the sport.[26]

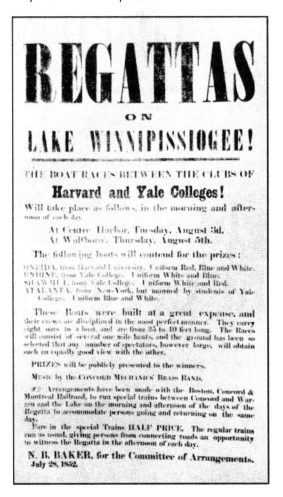

Figure 1.1 Flyer for first Harvard-Yale intercollegiate competition at Lake Winnipesaukee, 1852.

In the 1840s and 1850s, rowing was already established as a very popular sport for middle and upper classes across cities in the Northeast and near the Great Lakes, such as Boston, Baltimore, Pittsburgh, St. Louis, and Milwaukee, to name a few. Professional and amateur races thrived, bringing together crews from clubs, colleges, and other institutions.

Newspapers featured crew races on a regular basis and even participated as sponsors and organizers. It was in this context that the first Harvard-Yale race took place on August 3, 1852, when Yale students issued a formal challenge to their comrades at Harvard. The 1852 regatta was a public spectacle with sponsorships from a railroad company and newspapers. Among the public were members of some of the elite families in the country, including General Franklin Pierce, who would soon become president of the United States.[27]

A year later the Harvard-Yale contest included crews from other private colleges in the region, its popularity leading to it becoming an annual event. Representatives from Dartmouth, Columbia, Brown, Yale, and Harvard got together to initiate the organization of competitions between those institutions. In 1858 Harvard students proposed the creation of a college regatta association. In the 1860s the popularity of such contests reached new heights, particularly after the Harvard Crimson crew raced against Oxford on the Thames River in 1869, inspiring many other American undergraduates to initiate their own clubs and competitions.[28]

Intercollegiate regatta competitions were therefore the first organized college sport in American society, structured under complex rules and featured as events for the entertainment of large crowds. Crew athletes participated in elaborate training routines, with particular diet regimes and a full schedule of practice and exercise. After the Civil War, crew competitions intensified, leading clubs to increase and expand their training techniques, dietary regimes, and performance strategies. An inevitable step was to hire the best possible *advisor* or *coach* to take charge of the overall team-preparation process. Professional coaches trained student crews on a regular basis, trying to find competitive advantages against other teams. The ample coverage provided in the media on regatta by local and student newspapers and the public interest among students and nonstudents in the outcome only increased the social status of the sport across campuses and towns.

There were sixteen college teams affiliated with the American Rowing Association in 1870, with increasing competition to challenge Harvard's preeminence as the best team in the country. In 1871 the crew from Massachusetts Agricultural College defeated the Harvard Crimson crew, ending the supremacy of the first college sports dynasty.[29]

CREW OF 1897
Early Spring Practice on Lake Whitney

Figure 1.2 Yale Crew on Lake Whitney, 1897.

THE YALE RECORD CREW (1888)

Gill Wilcox James, sub Corbin Brewster Hartwell
Cross Woodruff Stevenson (Capt.) Carter
Thompson (Cox.)

Figure 1.3 Yale Record Crew, 1888.

Baseball

Although not as popular as rowing, baseball became a regular feature in college athletics in the late 1850s. On July 1, 1859, Amherst College and Williams College teams played the first intercollegiate ball game in Pittsfield, according to the Massachusetts rules of town ball. The final score was 73–32 in favor of Amherst. The match was the feature attraction in a two-day event that included a banquet, a chess match, and various social activities for the students of both institutions, and the local population in the *neutral* town of Pittsfield.

In the 1860s college baseball teams proliferated, expanding the scope of intercollegiate competitions to include the game. Harvard's first varsity ball team, the Crimson, was organized in 1862 and went undefeated for more than a decade. In 1870 the Crimson toured the United States, playing games against both college and professional teams. The baseball seasonal calendar (spring to early fall), however, seriously interfered with the organization of a regular season in the context of the traditional schedule for colleges (fall to winter). These incompatible schedules gave baseball only limited exposure at the college level. Baseball played a subordinated role in college sports despite its increasing popularity in nineteenth-century American society. Student organizations preferred to emphasize rowing as the ultimate sport for intercollegiate competition, although some prominent athletes would briefly participate in baseball activities in the spring and then switch to other sports in the fall.[30]

Track and Field

During and right after the Civil War, intercollegiate competitions expanded to include events beyond rowing. Once again inspired by the examples of the British schools and the Caledonian Games celebrated in the United Kingdom and the United States, American student organizations started the inclusion of running, jumping, and throwing contests, then called *athletics* and now *track and field*. These competitions took place right before, during, and/or around the regatta races. It was not unusual for some of the participating track and field athletes to come from the different rowing crews and classes.

Following the participation of other newspapers as sponsors of crew competitions, the *New York Herald* organized a race as a sideshow to the Saratoga Annual Regatta in 1873, and in 1876 the new Intercollegiate Association of Amateur Athletes of America started the organization of annual races at the New York Athletic Club, with cash prizes for the winning athletes.[31]

In the 1880s undergraduate associations fully embraced the *field-day meeting* format, a festival-like multisport event in which two schools would meet for regatta races, track and field contests, ball games, and in some cases football matches. A *field day* usually featured neighboring or rivaling institutions coming to an agreement to meet on a particular day and place, to compete at various levels and socialize.

C. H. Sherrill, Yale '89.   L. P. Sheldon, Yale,   F. S. Horan, Cambridge.   H. S. Brooks, Jr., Yale '86.
Some Track Athletes.

Figure 1.4 Yale Track athletes, 1886–1889.

Rugby

Football in the nineteenth-century college landscape was far and away from what is now. As was the case for crew, ball, and running, football became a formal sport in college athletics as students followed the examples of inter-school rugby games in the United Kingdom. Various examples of rugby games as interclass or intramural events had existed for private colleges on the Northeastern shores before the Civil War.[32] These games/events would take place on a yearly basis to emphasize the rivalries between different classes and to ritualize the arrival of new students on campus. Harvard and Yale led in such traditions but were certainly not the only institutions with football as an organized athletic activity. During and after the Civil War, rugby clubs and organizations underwent a significant expansion and evolved into formal meetings between two schools for a match arranged in accordance with conditions previously agreed on by the two student groups. The standard agreement was to either follow soccer association or rugby union rules as a general layout but, more importantly, to play the game according to the specific rules and traditions of the team providing the local field. Whereas in the United Kingdom the rules of rugby and soccer had become standardized in the 1860s, in the United States the customary tradition was to play according to house rules. Colleges and universities in American and Canadian institutions regularly scheduled a few football games in the fall following this house-rule format, a fact contributing to the ongoing debate as to which institution and which game between 1860 and 1875 was the first original college football game in the history of the sport.[33]

Sporting Fraternities

The most important social structure in the formation of college sports is the sporting fraternity. These social groups were vital in articulating recreational and leisure activities centered on physical exercise and athletic competitions.

Numerous sporting fraternities for young single male adults emerged on campuses across the country, particularly in the aftermath of the Civil War. Student organizations were at the core of a new physical culture environment in which sports played a decisive role in bringing together members of a class, college, or university against a common rival. Inspired by the closing of the American frontier, the successful struggle to maintain the Union against secession, and the increasing secularization of higher education, these groups envisioned sports to redefine an outdoor leisure life free from institutional supervision.

Outside institutions of higher education, similar sporting fraternities proliferated to form athletic clubs, sports associations, sports tournaments, and physical conditioning organizations, particularly in urban environments, where the influx of young single males was significantly reshaping the social fabric.[34]

Sport by sport, student organizations had complete control of intercollegiate competition, selection, training, and supervision of athletes. That does not mean these athletic activities were informal, improvised, or spontaneous. In fact, student athletics dedicated an enormous amount of time and effort to the organization, rules, and planning of each sport in question.

College sports developed into complex competitions in the second half of the nineteenth century as an initiative of young adult male student groups to shape a leisure and recreational culture beyond the supervision and control of school faculty and authorities.

In this effort, the projection of a masculine image that presented students as athletes and heroes before other students, alumni, rival students, and the public at large was certainly a defining element of the emerging sports culture. Crews, runners, ball players, and rugby athletes represented their institutions, fraternities, clubs, and themselves against rivals and the public, displaying a masculine ideal in which they were in control, asserting a manly identity based on strength, skills, and group membership.[35]

Sporting fraternities are consequently the main factor responsible for the birth of college sports in American society. As organizers of university life for the student community at large, these groups developed in sports a social space to establish connections among students, create hierarchies within the groups, and display masculine ideals for athletes and spectators.

Muscular Christianity

College sports developed in the context of a broader ideological movement in nineteenth-century American society, which envisioned physical activity and organized sports in new ways in response to the challenges that industrialization and urbanization represented for the traditional structures in family and patriarchal authority. The waves of industrialization covering Western Europe and North America in the nineteenth century generated profound changes in the composition of traditional communities and rural families. While the pillars of social life of preindustrial society were the parish church, the large extended family, and agricultural labor, the arrival of industrialization generated unprecedented social structures and a significant challenge to patriarchal and traditional hierarchies.

The Industrial Revolution generated a vast population movement through which individuals and families moved from the countryside to the urban areas. In the nineteenth century these processes followed an accelerated pace in the United Kingdom and the United States, where young adults found employment and better economic conditions. Such a demographic phenomenon raised concern among religious leaders and city authorities, as the number of boys and young adults in question were not considered to be raised properly in urban areas.[36]

The Muscular Christianity doctrine was a set of principles that identified supervised physical exercises, organized sports, and outdoor activities as the ideal method to regain parental control and ecclesiastic authority in the grooming of boys into men in urban areas. Originated in the United Kingdom in the first decades of the nineteenth century, Muscular Christianity became a widely popular ideology for physicians, reformers, school authorities, teachers, and politicians in the United States as the country entered an accelerated period of industrialization and urbanization.

The Muscular Christianity doctrine basically redefined the role of institutions in regard to physical exercise and organized sports. According to its principles, the consistent channeling of young boys into sports under institutional supervision was viewed not only as an ideal antidote against urban dangers but also a key to their successful transition into manhood and citizenship.[37]

The Muscular Christianity ideological platform identified organized sports as the best venue to lead young men into the traditional moral standards eroded by city life. Sports made boys into men by helping them reconnect with the natural virtues of countryside life and by reasserting parental control through institutional supervision to keep youth away from street life.

In 1844 Sir George Williams (1821–1905) founded a reading group for young Christian men in London, marking the start of the Young Men's Christian Association (YMCA) as an organization. The YMCA's primary mission was to provide leisure activities to young Christian men living in the rapidly growing urban areas. These single adult men, detached from the traditional sources of patriarchal and religious supervision, were considered a vulnerable population to the dangers of urban areas, namely drinking, gambling, and a wide range of illegal activities.[38]

The YMCA swiftly evolved into a multipurpose institution fully dedicated to meeting the spiritual and recreational needs of urban youth. Captain Thomas Sullivan started the first YMCA chapter in Massachusetts in 1851 after witnessing the organization at play in London. In the 1850s, YMCA chapters proliferated in cities from the Midwest to the Atlantic shore (Chicago, Illinois; Ann Arbor, Michigan; Washington, DC; and Providence, Rhode Island, among others). In 1858, Thomas W. Higginson, a writer, Unitarian minister, and abolitionist activist, published in the *Atlantic Monthly* an eloquent plea in favor of Muscular Christianity principles.[39] Other contemporary writers and ministers participated in the *Crusade for Sports in Schools*. Popular novels and writings by British authors Thomas Hughes and Charles Kingsley praised the benefits of sports in the development of a manly character, while American physician and Harvard Medical School professor Oliver Wendell Holmes advocated for athletics in the United States similar to those in Britain. Other writers, doctors, and reformers followed as advocates of the Muscular Christianity doctrine, changing the way in which clergy and school authorities looked at sports and making the argument for the inclusion of supervised physical activities in schools and colleges.[40]

A pivotal moment was the opening of the new YMCA facility in New York City in 1869, an impressive building that included a gymnasium.[41] The YMCA played a decisive role in the implementation of Muscular Christianity principles in the American urban landscape. Right after the Civil War, the vertiginous expansion of the YMCA's mission, principles, policies, and activities affected private and public colleges, as well as high schools and preparatory schools.

The YMCA's expansion after the Civil War created new social spaces for young men to live, practice sports, and socialize in urban areas. In Chicago, for example, the institution had more than two thousand members in the 1870s and was completely renovated in 1874 after two consecutive fires had destroyed the previous facilities in 1868 and 1871. By the 1890s Chicago's YMCA had several activities for youth, ranging from choir and reading the scriptures to dancing and musical bands. In terms of competitive sports, Chicago's YMCA had football, basketball, boxing, wrestling, track, and gymnastics teams. By the last decades of the nineteenth century, the YMCA had unquestionably become the most important urban institution for youth in the United States. In the 1870s the YMCA led the Intercollegiate Christian Movement and in the 1880s the foundation for the *Camping for Boys* programs (later to become the *Boy Scouts of America*).

Leading in summer activities for children and youth, high school clubs, sports associations, and even missionary trips to Japan, China, and other countries, the YMCA expanded and refined the principles of Muscular Christianity for entire communities across the country and abroad. The YMCA promoted organized sports and outdoor activities for boys around the nation and developed new physical activities and competitions to take place inside the gymnasium during winter. The two most successful examples of this innovative trend were organized basketball and volleyball. In 1891 basketball was officially born, as James Naismith, a chaplain and physical education instructor from Canada, redesigned callisthenic exercises to develop an indoor sport in the YMCA International Training School in Springfield, Massachusetts. Volleyball followed a similar process in its inception in 1895, designed by William G. Morgan, a physical education director in Holyoke, Massachusetts.

The YMCA mission to promote the "uplifting of young manhood" at spiritual, social, mental, and physical levels and to make the "salvation of young men" in urban areas a reality by providing a social space for leisure and recreational activities became a foundational development for the history of sports and school athletics in the nineteenth century.[42] In the 1890s the George Williams College trained YMCA future instructors, managers, and directors to spread the principles of Muscular Christianity and help American boys become men through sports. By the first decade of the twentieth century, the YMCA had participated in physical training for servicemen in the Spanish-American War (1898), programs for physical activities and sports for industrial workers, national swimming and lifesaving campaigns, father-and-son programs, and the foundation of the Boy Scouts of America.[43]

A fundamental distinction must be pointed out in the YMCA's outlook on the relationship between sports and adulthood according to gender. The YMCA encouraged the thought that athletics were ideal for boys because through competition and physical activities, they could reconnect with the "lost masculine" features no longer accessible to them in the urban environment: connection to nature, strenuous physical activity, and parental and religious supervision. In this patriarchal hierarchy, the relationship between sports and women had a completely different structure. The obvious outcome was that girls and young women would participate in sports only under strict supervision and that such activities be practiced only in moderation. While the first Ladies Christian Association dates back to 1858 in New York City, the first female boardinghouse in 1860, and the first Young Women's Christian Association in Boston in 1866, the first YWCA chapters that included sports only started in 1920.[44]

Conclusions

Intercollegiate athletics at their inception in the nineteenth century were the ultimate expression of student sporting communities in their drive to create a recreational and leisure lifestyle outside the limits of campus authorities and parental control. In this context, college sports began in American society as events and activities exclusively in the hands of student organizations, clubs, fraternities, and groups acting under little or no supervision from institutional authorities. College athletics reflected masculine ideals about student life, in-group identity, and college membership, and overall it reasserted the values of elite, privileged, white Anglo-Saxon Protestant families and communities in the Northeast.

Rowing became the first and most popular intercollegiate sport, organized by students on a regular basis in the Northeast first and then the Great Lakes region, followed by colleges across the country. These crew competitions took place in the middle of carefully planned and elaborate events that included other sports as well as a number of nonathletic social activities such as banquets, dinners, festivals, and parades.

Crew, baseball, running, and rugby constituted the first wave of intercollegiate sports produced by student sporting communities, a new social structure in which single white adult males socialized beyond the scope of institutional supervision by school officers and religious authorities. At the core of rowing events, student sporting communities reaffirmed gender, race, and class privileges as members of the American aristocratic elites. Rowing strongly reflected the rite of passage of attending college in preparation for assuming leading roles in the economic, social, and political spheres of elites nationwide.

While emphasizing the ludic elements of student life and the celebration of a bachelor subculture, rowing and other sports were conceived in this perspective as an apt metaphor for the transition between student and professional, youth and adult, and ultimately, boyhood and manhood.

Since their inception, college sports involved state-of-the-art training, dietary, and performance techniques, technologies, and principles, all reflecting the capitalist mentality prevalent in these elite sporting communities. Advisors, coaches, and trainers would develop and implement all possible methods to gain a competitive advantage against other institutions. Rather than being a digression from the dominant values and hierarchies regarding gender, class, and race rankings, college sports reflected and reproduced those rankings at the level of athletic competitions. The highly competitive ethos that shaped intercollegiate athletics from the very start echoed the elitist and capitalist mind-set characteristic of exclusive segregated colleges in American society.

Productivity, efficiency, competition, and ultimate success reflected in the final score were central components of sports organized by the socioeconomic elites of American capitalist society. Just like fair game symbolized fair trade and fair economic competition, the sports field was a powerful symbol of the market, the arena where the most prepared and most advanced would succeed.

Likewise, commercial and entrepreneurial principles were intrinsic elements of college sports from their inception. Monetary compensation for advisors and trainers was a common feature, just as the practice of charging spectators a monetary fee in exchange for sports entertainment. Private sponsorships, donations by alumni, and other sources of revenue were also present on a regular basis.

After the Civil War, intercollegiate sports underwent a significant expansion, featuring regular competitions in crew, baseball, track and field, and rugby. Following tradition and a business-oriented perspective, college sports were carefully organized by student competition committees that led the process of standardization of each athletic event and tournament, resulting in a very elaborate set of rules for each sport.

Embraced by the principles of Muscular Christianity, college sports started to be the subject of interest and supervision by college authorities, reformers, clergy, and physicians, who increasingly looked into ways to participate in the organization of athletic activities on campus. Contrary to common beliefs, intercollegiate athletics have little connection to the existence of gymnasiums in colleges and universities or to the development of physical education as an academic discipline in American institutions of higher education. While most elite institutions had a gymnasium and physical education classes on campus in the nineteenth century, intercollegiate competitions were effectively not connected to either of these two entities but instead were left entirely in the hands of student organizations. College athletics were consequently an expression of the vital leisure life developed on campus by student associations in elite colleges and universities, mostly but not exclusively on the Northeastern shores.

While school authorities looked down on college sports in general, in only few instances were they actually opposed to these events. Instead, such events were tolerated and conceived as one more manifestation of student life on campus. While the legal definition of *in loco parentis* (Latin for "in place of a parent") gave institutions of higher education in the nineteenth century the right and responsibility of regulating student behavior outside the classroom, which included every extracurricular activity, only rarely did college authorities intervene in the organization of intercollegiate athletics.

STUDY QUESTIONS

1. What are the connections between British and American intercollegiate competitions during the nineteenth century?

2. How did crew and baseball reflect the values of Muscular Christianity?

3. Prior to 1880, college authorities saw little value in student athletic activities but did not oppose them. Why?

4. What gender differences were strongly emphasized in the ideology of Muscular Christianity?

5. After the American Civil War, intercollegiate competitions progressed toward formal organizations and dramatically increased in number. Why?

6. Football rose to prominence only after the American Civil War. In which ways do you think these two processes are linked?

7. Student organizations had complete control of intercollegiate competitions, including the selection, training, and supervision of athletes. Why?

8. What was the role of the YMCA in the expansion of Muscular Christianity's principles?

9. Why were sports considered ideal for turning boys into men?

10. What commercial elements were present in the birth of intercollegiate athletics?

ADDITIONAL READINGS

Kimmel, Michael. *Manhood in America: A Cultural History.* New York: Free Press, 1996.

Lewis, Guy. "The Beginning of Organized Collegiate Sport." *American Quarterly* 22, no. 2 part 1 (Summer 1970): 222–29.

Lucas, Christopher J. *American Higher Education: A History*. 2nd ed. New York: Palgrave MacMillan, 2006.

Putney, Clifford. *Muscular Christianity: Manhood and Sports in Protestant America, 1880–1920*. Cambridge, MA: Harvard University Press, 2001.

Thelin, John R. *A History of American Higher Education*. 2nd ed. Baltimore: Johns Hopkins University Press, 2011.

Welch, Lewis Sheldon and Walter Camp. *Yale: Her Campus, Class-Rooms and Athletics*. With introduction by Samuel J. Elder. Boston: Page, 1900.

FIGURE CREDITS

Figure 1.1: Source: http://www.humankinetics.com/excerpts/excerpts/a-brief-historical-perspective-on-intercollegiate-athletics.

Figure 1.2: Lewis Sheldon Welch and Walter Camp, "Yale Crew on Lake Whitney, 1897," Her Campus, Class-rooms and Athletics, pp. 491. Copyright © 1900.

Figure 1.3: Lewis Sheldon Welch and Walter Camp, "Yale Record Crew 1888," Her Campus, Class-rooms and Athletics, pp. 466. Copyright © 1900.

Figure 1.4: Lewis Sheldon Welch and Walter Camp, "Yale Track Athletes, 1886-1889," Her Campus, Class-rooms and Athletics, pp. 585. Copyright © 1900.

American Football

A Preindustrial Ritual

Agricultural-based preindustrial societies generated games and sports for centuries before the arrival of organized football to schools in the United Kingdom and United States in the 1900s. Since the domestication of agriculture, preindustrial societies in Europe, Asia, and the Americas featured ball-kicking and ball-carrying competitions at various levels; hence the multiple origins of football and the many claims by historians that trace the birth of the sport to places like Imperial China, the ancient Greek city-states, the Mesoamerican ball game, or the late medieval Italian *calcio*.[45]

While some historians identify British schools as the inventors of football, in reality athletic competitions based on two goal zones with two opposing teams advancing a ball by different means had been a characteristic activity in preindustrial villages and parishes across various regions in the world.[46] A central element in these competitions was the celebration of the game in the middle of a religious event or town festivity. Representatives of parishes, towns, and villages would get together to kick and/or carry the ball with the ultimate goal of advancing it to the opponent's end zone, marked by trees, stones, natural ground lines, or other rural landmarks. The rules regarding scoring and the composition of the field and teams varied significantly according to town, region, and country.[47]

In ancient Mexico and Central America, many cities, such as Teotihuacan or Chichen Itza, had a specific field designated for a ball game. Players could advance the rubber ball by hitting it with a stick or propelling it through contact with any body part. Ball games took place to highlight religious ceremonies, where gambling on victory outcomes was allowed. Players were highly specialized athletes; the exaggerated accounts of these games indicate that the victors were sacrificed to the gods as the ultimate reward for athletic skill and prowess.[48]

In preindustrial Europe many communities had ball competitions for boys and young adults in the middle of carnivals, festivals, and religious ceremonies. Far from following standardized rules, each community had a set of informal regulations to be implemented according to customary laws and local tradition.[49]

In England and Scotland, communities in the countryside and villages frequently featured football competitions, sometimes called camping ball, camping, and hurling. The games were marked by a wide variety of rules in regard to field size, scoring, fouls, and number of players on each side. Authorities made numerous attempts to prohibit football, but the popularity of the game seemed to prevail against its detractors.[50]

In the eighteenth and nineteenth centuries, the game was central to student life in English secondary schools. Students at Eaton, Rugby, Westminster, and other institutions played football regularly, organizing the competition according to their own rules and preferences. In 1846 students from secondary schools organized a football match at Cambridge University, and in 1848 school representatives met again at Cambridge to formulate the first standardized rules for football, known as the Cambridge Code.[51]

A School Game

On November 6, 1869, a delegation from the College of New Jersey (now Princeton University) visited Rutgers College (now Rutgers University) to play a football match against the local student team. The following week it was the Rutgers delegation that traveled to Princeton to reciprocate the honor. These two matches are considered the first intercollegiate football games and markers of the first football season in American history.[52] A closer look into the 1869 games reveals these matches were completely different from what became American football only decades later. The first game took place according to Rutgers house rules, following the standards of other intercollegiate meetings and field days.[53] That meant each team had twenty-five players in the field, the ball was completely round, there was no running with the ball allowed, and each player could advance the football by kicking it or using any other body part, including the hands. There were no touchdowns, extra points, two-point conversions, field goals, or defensive safeties. Scoring was calculated by the number of times the ball went through the posts in the opposite team's end zone. Rutgers won 6 goals to 4.[54] In the second meeting, the rules changed to fit the tradition and standards of the local team and their house rules. This time Princeton defeated Rutgers 8 to 0. The competition rules were agreed on by each team's representatives on a game-by-game basis, making each meeting a unique contest in terms of scoring, penalties, number of players, and even field size.[55]

The 1869 Rutgers-Princeton games are also considered the first intercollegiate soccer matches and the first intercollegiate Rugby games in the United States. In reality these soccer/rugby matches did not follow the standardized rules of either rugby, established in 1845 and 1862, or the Soccer Association, established in 1862–1863, as they were implemented in the United Kingdom.[56]

Some scholars consider the ball game between McGill University and Harvard in 1874 to be the first intercollegiate football game, while others prefer to identify the 1875 game between Harvard and Yale as the first college football match. In support of the latter, it has been argued that the Harvard-Yale 1875 match followed rules that were different from both soccer and rugby. However, that was hardly the case. The final score was 4 goals to 1 in favor of the Yale Bulldogs, and there were an estimated two thousand paying spectators in attendance.[57]

Before the Civil War, college football was an organic element of student life on campus, a fall ritual to be followed by incoming students and a way to socialize members of different classes and organizations. College football was basically an after-class tradition organized as a game for ritualistic purposes and consisted of advancing the ball to the opposite goal by some means, which were locally defined by each college and university. However, football was not a standardized sport with a specific set of rules, nor was it an intercollegiate athletic competition. Unlike crew and other college sports, football did not follow the format of British institutions. Instead, each college had its own particular way of playing the game. Some institutions would follow the rules of soccer more than those of rugby, others would rely mostly on the rules of rugby, while most would combine the regulations of both sports, adding their own rules according to tradition and temperament.[58]

Harvard University students featured a traditional freshman-sophomore football game, "Bloody Monday," as part of the "rush" activities organized by and for the amusement of the upper class (junior and senior) students. According to legendary football figure and sports historian Parke H. Davis*:

> Upon the evening of the match, half-past six being the established hour, the upper classmen assembled and took seats up on a near-by fence. The two lower classes to the last man present were marshaled in two

---

* Parke H. Davis, Selections from *Football: The American Intercollegiate Game*. Copyright © 1911 by Scribner.

opposing lines, the sturdiest representative of the Freshmen being in the center of the line with the ball. At the signal both lines advanced on the run to the center of the Delta, where the Freshmen endeavored to force their champion with the ball through the Sophomores' ranks and onward to the line which the Sophomores defended. A copious amount of fisticuffs in this encounter not only was natural but was also permissible.[59]

The Bloody Monday tradition at Harvard persisted and became a crucial component of initiation rituals for incoming students, despite continuous efforts by school authorities and faculty to curb or prohibit it altogether. In 1860 Harvard authorities categorically banned the contest, triggering a strong student reaction marked by the celebration of a mock funeral of a football:

An ode specially composed for the occasion was then sung:

"Ah! Woe betide the luckless time
When manly sports decay,
And football stigmatized as crime
Must sadly pass away!

"Beneath this sod we lay you down
This sign of glorious fight
With dismal groans and yells we'll drown
Your mournful burial rite!

"For 'sixty-three will never see
Such cruel murder done
And not proclaim the deed of shame.
No! Let's unite as one!"

The grave then was closed and a tablet erected bearing the following inscription:

HIC JACET
FOOTBALL FIGHTUM
Obiit July 2, 1860.
Aet. LX Years
RESURGAT[60]

Despite the ban, Harvard students resurrected the tradition on April 21, 1872, with a contest between the 1874 and 1875 classes.

Students at Yale regularly organized a similar rush/football tradition to establish authority and precedence over incoming classes:

To New Haven's Green on the afternoon of the fray came the Sophomores in fantastic and painted faces. The Freshmen under the guidance
of the upper classmen were withdrawn to one side and formed into a
great, solid, V-shaped mass, with the most gigantic Freshman of the class
carrying the ball and buried within the wedge. At the signal this mass
started to plough heavily across the Green. A corps of picked Sophomores
threw themselves upon its apex and their comrades fell upon its flanks
in a fierce endeavor to reach and capture the ball.[61]

The interclass contest followed elaborate rituals in the organization of the
event, from the formal invitation and challenge to the specific game rules
and appointment of judges.[62] In 1857, for example, a written challenge was
posted in the school Lyceum:

*"Sophomores: The class of '61 hereby challenges the class of '60 to a game of
football, best two in three.*

"On behalf of the Class,
> *"R.L. Chamberlain*
> *"James W. McLane*
> *"A. Sheridan Burt*

Before the day was done upon the door of Athenaeum appeared '60's reply:

> *"Come!*
> *And like sacrifices in their trim,*
> *To the fire eyed naiads of smoky war*
> *All hot and bleeding will we offer you.'*

"To Our Youthful Friends of the Class of '61.
> *We hereby accept your challenge to play the noble and time honored game
> of football and appoint 2½ o'clock P.M., on Saturday, October 10, 1857, the
> football grounds at the time and place."[63]*

In a parallel development to the efforts to eradicate the tradition at Harvard, Yale authorities and New Haven ordinances prohibited football at the
institution in the 1860s.[64] Despite institutional efforts, students resurrected
the tradition with a vigorous momentum in the 1870s. After the Civil War,
as the expansion in intercollegiate competitions started to include meetings
between rugby clubs games would follow the house rules of the home university. More often than not the sport was called rugby, not football. Each
institution would have its own set of regulations for the field size, boundaries, scoring system, advancing rules, time length, number of players, and
referees.[65]

In the 1870s rugby teams proliferated in the Ivy League and later in other private and public universities. Yale's first official rugby team dates from 1872. In 1873 Princeton, Columbia, Rutgers, and Yale were the first institutions to make an effort to standardize the game and create a general set of rules to be followed by all competitors. Student organizations from Princeton, Columbia, Harvard, and Rutgers created the first Intercollegiate Football Association in 1876. Field sizes underwent a remarkable reduction in length, from 140 or 150 yards to 120, including a gradual reduction in width as well. When Yale joined the association in 1879, the development of American football in elite college institutions had reached a decisive moment.[66]

1880s Time and Motion

In the 1880s significant transformations reshaped football competitions between Northeastern universities. Trying to counteract Harvard's long-established hegemony in sports, students at Yale and Princeton made systematic efforts to prepare better teams and challenge their traditional rivals. In this context the transformation of rugby into American football unfolded as the competition reached new levels in specialization and functional rationalization.

Walter Camp, a Yale student in the 1870s and a football advisor or coach in the 1880s, led a series of changes in the game rules to increase the ability to plan offensive and defensive schemes in advance and to reduce spontaneity and improvisation in the gridiron. As a member of the rules committee for the Intercollegiate Football Association, Camp proposed a series of new rules to standardize the competition and increase the opportunities to include more-developed team plays and game plans.

Unsatisfied with the Rugby Union Rules and clearly not happy with the soccer association developments in the United Kingdom, American college football teams on the Northeastern Seaboard made various attempts to find a more acceptable version of the sport with uniform and standardized rules for every match and field. The football programs at Yale and Princeton led a new wave to change the game in a similar fashion to the ways in which British cricket had evolved into American baseball.[67] With Camp as the engineer and founding father of these transformations, college football in the 1880s adopted three radical changes to make football in American colleges different from both rugby and soccer.

Figure 2.1 Walter Camp as Yale Captain, 1878–1879.

1. Outlet of Scrimmage

Camp considered the scrimmage line the backbone of American football. The scrimmage line rule allowed teams to design plays in advance and plan in detail each individual member's role in the play. For Camp, this innovation was the main difference between rugby union and what he called American football:

> What is therefore, in the English game a matter of considerable chance is "cut-and-dried" in the American game; and the element of chance being eliminated, opportunity is given for the display in the latter game of far more skill in the development of brilliant plays and carefully planned maneuvers.[68]

2. Interference

The second radical change in the Rugby Union Rules adopted by Yale and its opponents was called interference, which basically allowed the players on the offensive team to assist the ball-carrying runner and "break a path for him or shoulder off would-be tacklers."[69] Offensive blocking could be designed and choreographed in advance, making runs less spontaneous or improvised.

3. First and Five Rule

Originally called the *block game rule* or *block*, this rule allowed offensive teams to maintain continuous possession of the ball for a set of block of plays (three) and to extend the drive by rewarding the team with additional blocks every time it could advance five or more yards. A first-and-five block of three plays would be granted when the team moved the ball ahead the required distance:

> I refer to the "block game." This method of play, which consisted in a succession of "downs" without advance and without allowing the opponents any chance of securing possession of the ball … a rule was introduced making it incumbent upon a side to advance the ball five yards or retreat with it ten in three "downs." If this advance or retreat were not accomplished, the ball went at once into the possession of the opponents. Never did a rule in any sport work so immediate and satisfactory reform as did this five-yard rule.[70]

Camp envisioned the block game as a device to facilitate a more precise system to prepare offensive plays on the one hand. On the other hand, the first-and-five rule also enhanced the defensive team's ability to reposition and neutralize offensive plays by anticipating their development based on the analysis of particular formations. The best defense began with the "reading" of each offensive formation and the development of a defensive formation that could prevent the coming play from progressing altogether:

> We now realize that the best defence does not consist in planning how to stop a man after he has obtained a fair start towards the goal, but in throwing all available force up against him before he can get free of the forward line.[71]

The changes in football rules created a more complex, faster, more physical, and more violent game, and they placed the success of each play not exclusively on the individual abilities of the best players but on the synchronized and collective efforts of each and every individual in the field. In order to maximize productivity in the game, each player had an individual and specific role to deploy in each play in the field.

Camp also provided a detailed account of the responsibilities and attributes that each player in the game should have according to his position in the field. Tackle, end rusher, guard, center or snapback, halfback, and quarterback all had specific and particular responsibilities for team performance.

The entire series of motions, therefore, which go to make up a well-performed kick should be in the coach's mind just as the separate parts of an oarsman's stroke are in the boating man's mind when coaching a crew.[72]

The specialization of each position in the field, or as Camp put it, "the division of players," came with an increasingly dominant role of the coach, who became the most important element in the playmaking decision process. Coaches and captains developed plays to be rigorously practiced and executed, in which every position had a unique and specific role to perform. Football developed a sophisticated system of signals to communicate each play to the team in advance.

To-day the teams which meet to decide the championship are brought up to the execution of at least twenty-five different plays, each of which is called by a certain distinct signal of its own.[73]

The team captain or quarterback was assigned the role of communicating the next play by using coded words, hand signals, and numerical combinations.

Taking the same signals as a basis, the first, or signal for the right half-back to try on the left end, was one-two-three- the sum of these numbers is six. Take that, then, as the key to this signal, and any numbers the sum of which equals six will be a signal for this play. For instance, three-three, or four-two, two-three-one- any of these would serve to designate this play.

... He [the coach] should remember that training ought to be a preparation by means of which his men will at a certain time arrive at the best limits of their muscular strength and activity, at the same time preserving that equilibrium most conducive to normal health. Such a preparation can be accomplished by the judicious use of the ordinary agents of well-being—exercise, diet, sleep, and cleanliness.[74]

Walter Camp

Walter Camp was born in New Haven, Connecticut, in 1859. Camp's father was a schoolteacher with considerable properties in New Haven and nearby towns. Coming from a privileged family in the area, Camp attended an elite grammar school with a national reputation. Camp went to Yale University, where he played various sports dating from 1877. After graduation, Camp spent some time at the Yale Medical School while participating as football coach. During Camp's tenure, Yale football teams became the most dominant squads in college sports, overcoming both Harvard and Princeton and thereby establishing the first dynasty in the history of football. Camp's astonishing success turned him into a public figure and authority on fitness, youth education, sports, and modern training.

During World War I, Camp was chair of Training Camp Activities for the US Navy. He wrote more than twenty books on sports, physical training, education, and other topics. After dropping out from Yale Medical School, Camp entered the labor market in New York City, where he briefly worked in the Manhattan Watch Company. In 1883, he joined the New Haven Clock Company. In 1886, he became manager in the sales department and, in 1893, assistant treasurer. In 1902, he became the corporation's treasurer and general manager and one year later its president, a position he left in 1923.

The New Haven Clock Company was founded in 1853 by Hiram Camp, a relative, but was far from a small family business. In the 1860s, the company employed more than three hundred workers and sold more than 170,000 clocks per year. In the 1880s, when Camp joined the corporation, the clock factory had more than six hundred employees, including more than eighty children. The enterprise sold clocks all over the world and had sales offices in the United Kingdom and Japan. The large-scale production of clocks and watches featured a variety of products, including affordable pocket watches. Camp's presidency in the corporation was marked by the introduction of modern manufacturing processes and a further expansion in the product line to offer wristwatches for mass consumption. During Camp's tenure the company consolidated its position as one of the largest clock-manufacturing businesses in the world, if not the largest.

Method, Not Man: Time Management in American Football

Camp's principles to revolutionize football followed a functional rationalization inspired by the radical transformations in large-scale American manufacturing sectors, from the meatpacking industry to the assembly lines in the production of automobiles. The modernization wave in the manufacturing industries had created more-efficient, less-expensive, and highly organized systems and processes based on segmentation, mechanization, and specialization.[75]

Camp's innovations had turned a school game into a highly elaborate competition that mirrored the organizational structures of American industrial life and the capitalist fantasy of having human labor operating as the most advanced machine.

Figure 2.2 Walter Camp: American football player, coach, and sports writer, 1900.

The 1883 modern scrimmage line, the first-down-and-five possession rule, and the three-downs-to-advance modification effectively eradicated the old rugby structure of football and gave birth to American football. Altogether, these changes allowed for the reorganization of offense and defense teams for each of the plays in question, created the quarterback and center positions, and made the game less fluid, less spontaneous, faster, more violent, and highly efficient.

The fragmentation of the game in downs mirrored the segmentation of labor in the manufacturing sector and other industries, while the arrival of quarterback and center as key positions in the offensive development echoed the principle of rational specialization of labor to maximize efficiency. The continuous possession system by which offensive teams would be rewarded with three more opportunities to advance if they could accomplish the "production goal" of five or more yards is also a sports interpretation of the productivity values in large-scale manufacturing systems.

Every By-Product Organized to Its Last Possibility

Walter Camp and Yale innovations to the sport of rugby were the driving force in the metamorphosis of the competition and its evolution into a completely different sport, run by time, efficiency, productivity, and functional rationalization. In this process, the incorporation of scientific management principles and systems from cutting-edge capitalist technologies produced a highly specialized team competition in which spontaneity and fluid play were replaced by carefully planned and practiced plays and choreographed team moves. Teams were supposed to perform like high-quality clocks, because clocks reflected some of the most refined, precise, and technologically advanced machineries of this period. Synchronization and specialization became key principles in the overall development of successful football teams and later other college athletics altogether.

Football players were no longer juvenile improvisers who relied on natural speed and strength; rather, they were regarded as carefully produced machine parts and movements needed to execute play-by-play, the system engineered by coaches to increase speed, strength, efficiency, and productivity. *Method, not Man*, Camp's motto, became the standard of the sport as it mirrored the industrial expectations of turning men into sophisticated machine parts.[76]

By the end of the nineteenth century, football had clearly transformed the landscape of college sports not only in achieving a central space as the preeminent fall competition, but also in developing training, dietary, and lifestyle routines that fit the new industrial standards of sport athletics in American universities.

The innovations brought into the game by Camp and the Yale dynasty in the 1880s and 1890s turned a version of student rugby into a highly specialized, sophisticated, and complex new sport played by athletes trained, fed, and monitored under new standards centered on time management, productivity, and efficiency, all dear principles in the formation of capitalist elites.

"The Things That a White Man and a Square Man Should Do"[77]

Walter Camp developed and propagated a new philosophical vision for the benefits of football on students and youth in general: The sport would help them in their transition from boys into men. As an apostle of the Muscular

Christianity doctrine, Camp firmly believed that the practice of football and physical exercise in general would facilitate the reconnection between boys and nature that urbanization and industrialization had made difficult if not insurmountable. In several writings, Camp advocated for physical exercises and organized sports for youth.

In Camp's view, students in private colleges in the Northeast should pursue the cultivation of fitness and the participation in college sports as a primary duty in their obligations as future leaders and as an inescapable obligation to contribute to their university or alma mater.[78] College sports were no longer a student recreational activity but a central element in the collective journey into manhood and a paramount contribution to the reputation and glory of the university itself.

In partnership with the publisher D. Appleton and Company, Camp disseminated these values and principles by writing various fictional stories for college and school, as well as informational pamphlets on physical exercise. Fictional stories like *Danny the Freshman, Danny Fists, Captain Danny, Old Ryerson, Jack Hall at Yale,* and *The Substitute* featured young boys and school lads finding in sports and physical exercise values to successfully transition into manhood.

Danny the Freshman (1915) begins with Daniel Phipps Jr. receiving an admission letter from Yale University. The night before his departure, Danny has a conversation with his father, who provides prudent advice:

> "In the first place, at Yale you'll be your own boss. There'll be no ten-o'clock bell, and nobody to report to, and so long as you obey the laws and keep up with your studies, you'll be your own master. The whole thing looks like great freedom, doesn't it? Well, you'll find before your four years are out that every bit of that freedom has some responsibility attached to it.
>
> The written laws of the college are plain. It is the unwritten laws that make or break you. There are the traditions of the men themselves. They are something like school customs with this difference—at school there is a chance to live down mistakes rather easily; at college it is a much harder job, and sometimes a man suffers for a mistake all through his course. And yet Danny, these unwritten laws are not hard to understand. They involve nothing but the things that a white man and a square man should do, anyway."
>
> Danny drew a deep breath: "I understand, sir."
>
> "Good! Now, Danny, the important thing is this—Yale demands something of every man who goes through. It's a sentiment. But it isn't talked about. It isn't hauled out so that people can scoff at it. Yale demands

that a man do something—athletics, debating, glee club, something. Get that idea fixed. Got it?"

"Yes, sir."

Mr. Phipps smiled. "I guess yours will be athletics?"

"Football and baseball," said Danny, and added modestly: "If I can make it."[79]

As in other manuscripts published under Camp's name, some authored by ghostwriters according to Camp's standards and supervision, the protagonists would discover in school and college sports intrinsic values in the masculine identity of the modern white American man: initiative, loyalty, discipline, sacrifice, hard work, aggressiveness, and so on.[80] Young protagonists would overcome various obstacles in their journey to full manhood and peer recognition as leaders of their class.

> When we call a boy a thoroughbred, we know he is a boy who is high-spirited, plucky, courageous, and strong. Every boy wants to be the type that is described by these expressions. To make himself fit, he must follow the precepts of health and of morality. Every boy is eager to stand well with his fellows, to be an aid to his team in its sports, to be an individual champion, to play fair and to play well. These things are possible under a course of care and self-discipline not difficult of attainment by any youth. ... If, however, a boy has the wish to excel, he takes on a contract which involves patience, self-control, persistence, and hard work. No boy or man ever made himself a leader in sports, or in life, without doing a great deal of hard work which at times seemed to be drudgery. No one comes to the top without making certain sacrifices. It is not an easy road, but it is an eminently satisfactory road, because it leads to the desired end.[81]

Camp and his generation perceived the athletic hegemony of Ivy League teams in the national landscape as a manifestation of the higher status of white and particularly white Anglo-Saxon Protestant men in the racial hierarchy. Reflecting the values prevalent in many of his contemporaneous peers, Camp envisioned college sports as an expression of the mental and physical superiority of the white race over other groups. College sports therefore arrived at the turn of the twentieth century, intrinsically linked to the ideological values of the country's socioeconomic elites, deeply attached to new notions affirming of racial hierarchies, reasserting white privilege, and defining man-making venues for the new times. Under Walter Camp and the Yale dynasty, college football became the most important college competition nationwide and a powerful metaphor for success, white masculinity, and privilege in American capitalist society.

Such has been the history of intercollegiate football. It has been only a sport, but its gridirons have been the training-grounds upon which men have been made. Where are the players whose names appear in the stories of these games? They are at the head of great business enterprises. They are occupying posts of distinction and honor in our government. They are presiding as judges in our courts, as presidents and professors in our institutions of learning. Transferred from the mimic battles of the lines of lime, they are leading our armies and commanding our warships. Clergymen, merchants, lawyers, authors, doctors, inventors, manufacturers, whatever and wherever they are, they are pursuing their vocations with courage, solving their problems with wisdom, and treating their competitors with honor, worthy soldiers from a worthy school.[82]

STUDY QUESTIONS

1. Describe Walter Camp's modification of the Rugby Union Rules named *outlet of scrimmage.*

2. Describe the modification of the Rugby Union Rules named *interference.*

3. Describe the *block game system* and the *five-yard rule.*

4. Describe the role of the quarterback in *American football.*

5. Discuss the dietary regimes for football players and college athletes presented by Walter Camp.

6. For what reasons were eating, drinking, sleeping, exercising, and cleanliness to be regulated?

7. What do you think was the overall impact of these rule changes on the game?

8. According to Camp, what are the reasons for the evolution from English rugby to rugby football or American rugby?

9. Describe the characteristics of functional rationalization in college football.

10. Discuss the connections between functional rationalization in college football and the class origins of Yale and Ivy League students.

11. Discuss the links between functional rationalization and commercialization in college football.

12. Discuss the principles of specialization and information in Camp's view of coaching teams.

13. Yale football teams embraced the principle of "every by-product organized to its last possibility." Explain.

14. Discuss the links between American elite families and Yale and Harvard athletic organizations.

15. Discuss the influence of social class values on Ivy League college football.

ADDITIONAL READINGS

Camp, Walter. *American Football*. New York: Harper, 1891.

Davis, Parke H. *Football: The American Intercollegiate Game*. New York: Scribner, 1911.

Powel, Harford. *Walter Camp, the Father of American Football: An Authorized Biography*. Boston: Little, Brown, 1926.

Westby, David L., and Allen Sack. "The Commercialization and Functional Rationalization of College Football: Its Origins." *Journal of Higher Education* 47, no. 6 (1976): 625–47.

FIGURE CREDITS

Figure 2.1: Source: https://commons.wikimedia.org/wiki/File:Walter_Camp_-_Project_Gutenberg_eText_18048.jpg.

Figure 2.2: Source: https://www.loc.gov/item/2014682621/.

3

King Football

Introduction

In the early twentieth century, there were two transformative developments that played a crucial role in the shaping of college football as a spectacle for mass entertainment. In 1903 the first steel-and-concrete stadium in the country was constructed under the patronage of Harvard University alumni.[83] Two years later formal committees led by college presidents were created to reform football, which eventually lead to the formation of the NCAA. The formal committees came as a result of a wide variety of issues regarding the organization of the sport and in response to an urgent need to regulate the increasing violence inherent in college football competitions. The changes implemented in the 1880s in college football had effectively created a new sport, where the elaborate planning of each play generated faster, stronger, and more efficient moves across the field. An unanticipated outcome in these transformations was the increase in violence and injuries in the sport. As coaches choreographed plays step-by-step for every individual trying to break through the defensive line with the maximum possible strength and speed, physical contact in the field not only increased but also became a threat to the players' physical integrity, provoking at times lethal consequences.

Figure 3.1 Western Championship between Chicago Maroons and Michigan Wolverines, Marshall Field, Chicago, Illinois, November 1905.

In 1905 US president Theodore Roosevelt summoned the football coaches of Harvard, Princeton, and Yale to the White House with the purpose of finding new ways to curb the sports brutality and protect the amateur status of college athletics. Newspapers in New York and Chicago highlighted the violent nature of football during the 1905 season, presenting lists of injuries and casualties in high school and college, while magazines like *Collier's* and *McClure's* featured stories on the sport's unethical standards and brutality.[84]

On Thanksgiving Day 1905, a tragedy that tipped the scales unfolded in the game between Union College and New York University (NYU) in Manhattan. Harold R. Moore, a nineteen-year-old right halfback player for Union College, was knocked unconscious after his head was slammed to the ground while tackling a runner. Unable to recover or regain consciousness, Moore was taken to Fordham Hospital and declared dead within six hours.[85] The incident received wide coverage in the press nationwide, and new calls to change or terminate the sport proliferated.

NYU chancellor Henry M. McCracken sent a telegram to Harvard University president Charles W. Eliot, inviting him to a meeting of college and university presidents "to undertake the reform or abolition of football."[86] As the telegram indicated, McCracken's national conference had two clearly divided camps, one in favor of making the sport less violent and the other committed to the termination of the sport in higher education.

The conference proceedings continued into 1906, and while the pro-reformation party seemed to gain momentum, various institutions (such as Columbia, Stanford, Northwestern, and California) decided to terminate their football programs unilaterally. The 1905–1906 conference created new rules for the sport and a new organization in charge of college football and eventually of college athletics altogether. Presidents of colleges and universities were to be in charge of organizing and designing the rules for the sport, displacing student organizations and athletic committees formed by students and alumni. Intercollegiate competitions became an affair in the hands of the institutional authorities. In 1910 this new association of institutional authorities officially became the NCAA.

NCAA Rules

In the middle of the debates about football reform, the Big Nine (now the Big Ten) Conference agreed on a set of changes to address the current crisis: the reduction of games per season to a maximum of five, strict rules of eligibility (three years and for undergraduate students only), a one-year residence rule before athletic participation, and finally, appointments of faculty or instructional staff only to football coach with paid salary. In general, these Big Nine rules were adopted by the national conference in April 1906.

The priority of eliminating brutality in football was not as easy to tackle as the issue of eligibility. By the spring of 1906 the American Intercollegiate Football Rules Committee devised a new set of rules to reduce body contact in the field and make the game less violent altogether.

The forward pass and the first-down-and-ten rules were two of the most radical changes in the regulation of the game. Allowing teams to pass the ball forward would significantly spread the action in the field while reducing the number and times players had contact at the scrimmage line. While being accepted under a number of restrictions and limitations, the new forward pass rule created the opportunity to diversify offensive plays and reduce the volume of traffic and contact at the frontline.

The first-and-ten rule would give offensive teams three chances to advance ten yards, instead of the traditional first-and-five rule implemented by Yale in the 1880s. The increase in the space to gain three more chances for continuing the drive would also encourage teams to spread in the field and pass the ball forward. The first-and-ten rule transformed offensive schemes based on strength and momentum into more versatile plays based on synchronization, speed, and skill. A few years later, the rules committee changed the number of downs from three to four in each drive.

Overall, the new rules from 1906 created an opportunity to make the game faster, with more scoring opportunities resulting in higher scores. While football was still a game to be fought and decided in the trenches, the innovations allowed for a more diverse set of offensive formations and more sophisticated strategies to attack and defend. Coaches, players, and fans would soon notice the differences in the game, which had become faster, more agile, and more appealing to wider audiences.

Stadium Revolution

At the dawn of the twentieth century, college football became the first sports spectacle designed for mass consumption. In 1903 the inauguration of Harvard Stadium represented the first step in the arrival of football as a public phenomenon. Harvard Stadium was the first massive structure of reinforced concrete and steel in the world, the first large permanent college sports arena, and the largest sports venue in the entire country. Built as the twenty-fifth anniversary gift from the class of 1879, the stadium represented the ultimate consolidation of football as a central and permanent feature in the institution's campus life. Loosely inspired by the classic Hellenic tradition, Harvard Stadium placed American football at the center of collegiate sports in a landscape evocative of the ancient Greek games, while football players and other college athletes were framed as and elevated to the status of Hellenic heroes.

Figure 3.2 Harvard-Dartmouth football game at Harvard Stadium, 1903.

The Yale Bowl, inaugurated in 1914, was the first venue designed in an oval shape to provide the best view for the highest number of spectators. Announced as the "largest amphitheater built since the Roman Coliseum,"[87] the Yale Bowl became an instant landmark on campus and represented a majestic venue in direct competition with Harvard Stadium. While the stadium's seat capacity certainly did not reflect the student enrollment or the total number of graduates from the institution between 1718 and 1914, dead or alive, the colossal dimensions of the Yale Bowl redefined the stage where football contests would be displayed.

As in the case of Harvard Stadium, there was a significant mismatch between the stadium capacity and the number of students enrolled. According to the school's historical statistics, enrollment in the 1913–14 academic year was 3,310, while all degrees conferred between 1900 and 1913 were 9,729 in total.[88]

The third Ivy League power, Princeton, also joined the stadia revolution in college athletics and inaugurated Palmer Stadium in 1914 with a capacity for 45,750 spectators. Harvard, Yale, and Princeton, therefore, initiated the largest sports infrastructure in modern history, featuring college football as a phenomenon for thousands of spectators and mass consumption.

In 1914 the University of Wisconsin developed plans to build Camp Randall Stadium, a small steel-and-concrete permanent stadium, which was inaugurated in 1917. After World War I large state universities made substantial investments to provide their institutions with football stadiums that could compete and/ or outperform the Yale Bowl: Memorial Stadium in Kansas (1920), California Memorial Stadium (1923), Memorial Stadium in Illinois (1923), Memorial Stadium in Nebraska (1923), Texas Memorial Stadium (1924), Ohio Stadium (1924), Michigan Stadium (1927), and so on. In the fewer than twenty-five years between the construction of Harvard Stadium and Michigan Stadium, college football in the United States had developed the largest sports infrastructure complex in the entire world, with several stadiums, each with a capacity of several thousand fans, constituting an unprecedented development in the history of sports entertainment. No other sport could compete with "king football" at the level of stadiums and fans. The MLB, for instance, had undergone a similar transformation with the opening of its first steel-and-concrete park in Philadelphia's Shibe Park (1909) and culminating in the construction of Yankee Stadium (1923), but most parks in the major leagues could only house thirty thousand spectators. While the inauguration of Yankee Stadium generated reports of over seventy thousand fans, in reality the facility could only allocate close to sixty thousand. College football stadiums have been, even to this date, the largest sports facilities in the country. Beyond the planning and investments by large public universities, football contests between colleges drew the attention of cities and sports entrepreneurs with a special interest in participating in this new form of mass entertainment. In Chicago the opening of Municipal Grant Park Stadium (1919), renamed Soldier Field in 1925, regularly featured college football matches with powerful teams in the 1920s: Notre Dame, Army, Navy, Michigan, and Wisconsin. The opening of the Los Angeles Memorial Coliseum (1923) and the Rose Bowl (1923) in Southern California followed a similar strategy in featuring college matches as the main events for each venue.

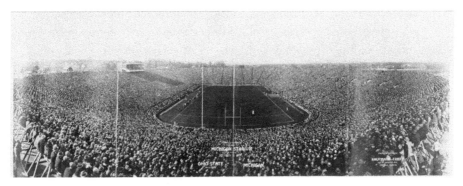

Figure 3.3 Michigan Stadium opening, Ohio State Buckeyes versus Michigan Wolverines, 1927.

Inaugurated on October 1, 1927, Michigan Stadium was the largest football stadium and the largest sports venue in the United States and the entire world. On its dedication on October 22 of that year, with the Michigan vs. Ohio State contest, the stadium's attendance exceeded eighty-four thousand fans. Continuing to push the envelope, in 1930 Michigan Stadium was the first sports venue to feature electronic scoreboards at each end of the field.

The financing of stadiums by big state universities posed a significant challenge. Public universities had definitely larger alumni bases than elite institutions of the Ivy League, but the former lacked the financial power and high economic status of the latter. Unlike Harvard Stadium, no single alumni class could afford the building of a massive steel-and-concrete sports venue.

To address this challenge, the Board in Control of Athletics at the University of Michigan designed a unique strategy to finance the construction of its stadium: the release of three thousand bonds to be sold at $500 each in order to raise $1.5 million.*

> United States of America
> State of Michigan
> Board in Control of Athletics
> No. 2999 $500.00
> University of Michigan
> 3% State Tax Exempt Bonds 3%
> CARRYING PREFERRED SEAT PURCHASE PRIVILEDGE
>
> KNOW ALL MEN BY THESE PRESENTS, That the BOARD IN CONTROL OF ATHLETCS of the University of Michigan, a corporation organized and existing under and by virtue of the Laws of the State of Michigan, hereby acknowledges itself indebted, and for value received, promises itself to pay the bearer the sum of FIVE HUNDRED DOLLARS ($500.00) lawful money of the United States of America on the fifteenth day of October, A.D. 1926 at the Ann Arbor Savings Bank of Ann Arbor, Michigan, with interest thereupon until paid, of three percent, per annum, payable annually on the fifteenth day of October of each year from the date hereof, on presentation and surrender of the proper interest coupons attached as they severally become due, and for the prompt payment of the principal and interest of this bond of the series of which it forms a part, the full faith, credit and resources of the Board in Control of Athletics of the University of Michigan are irrevocably pledged.

---

* Bentley Historical Library, "Carrying Preferred Seat Purchase Privilege." Copyright © by University of Michigan.

This bond is one of a series of three thousand bonds of like date and tenor aggregating one million five hundred thousand dollars in amount authorized to be issued by the Board in Control of Athletics of the University of Michigan and in pursuance of a resolution of said board.

The bonds are redeemable at any interest bearing date and par and accrued interest to day of redemption on thirty days notice. Annual redemption of one twentieth of the bonds sold is guaranteed, the bonds thus to be called to be determined by lot. Redemption of the entire issue is guaranteed within twenty years from date.

Each bond is to carry with it the privilege and right to purchase, by the owner of record in the office of the Board in Control of Athletics of the University of Michigan, at regular prices, two tickets for each foot ball game played at Ann Arbor, Michigan, in which the University of Michigan team participates, and for which reserved seats are sold, these seats to be located, in a special, reserved section within the thirty yard lines on either side of the field. The ticket privilege is to begin with the foot ball season of 1927 and continue through the foot ball season of 1936, a period of ten years and further within the life of the bonds to all holders of bonds not retired within the first ten years. The holders of bonds retired by lot at any time before or during 1936 shall be entitled to purchase reserve seat tickets as above provided up to and including the foot ball season of 1936.

However, the Board in Control of Athletics reserves the right to call or retire any bond or bonds held by any person or persons whenever in the judgment of said Board in Control it is for the best interest of itself or of the University of Michigan that the ticket purchasing privilege accompanying such bond or bonds be terminated, on the payment of the principal and interest accrued at the time of such call to the owner of such bond declaring the purchase privilege of tickets to be terminated therewith.

These bonds are transferable and the right to purchase tickets as above provided for is likewise transferable with the bond, providing notice of such transfer in writing shall be given the Board in Control of Athletics.

IN WITNESS WHEREOF, the Board in Control of Athletics of the University of Michigan has, on this fifteenth day of October, A.D. 1926 caused its corporate seal to be affixed hereto, this bond to be signed by its Chairman and Secretary, and has also caused fac-simile signatures of its Chairman and Secretary to be affixed on each of the coupons hereto annexed.

BOARD IN CONTROL OF ATHLETICS
UNIVERSITY OF MICHIGAN
BY (Chairman Signature)
BY (Secretary Signature).[89]

As several universities nationwide built stadiums with capacity for forty thousand to seventy thousand seats, the institutionalization of athletic boards with broad powers to successfully finance the construction represented a new step in a de facto incorporation of sports into the university's mission. Athletic boards, departments, or committees expanded their authority, powers, and influence to finance these unprecedented projects. The building of a sports venue in the middle of campuses nationwide represented the ultimate marriage between universities and athletics.

The financing of large sports stadiums by public universities followed not only the need to abandon the hazardous model of building wooden stands, but also institutional goals to make the stadium a symbol of the status and success of the university nationwide. College authorities engaged in these large sports infrastructure projects with the expectation of enhancing the public image and prestigious status of their respective institutions. Stadiums therefore became symbols of success for the sponsoring institutions and sources of pride for the student communities and the state populations. Combining private funds, public subsidies, state loans, individual donations, and fund-raising drives, public universities successfully built the largest sports infrastructure in the country and the world.

Football stadiums consequently became instant landmarks for state and regional pride and exemplary monuments to the crowning of college football as a sport for mass consumption. The football stadium became a central feature in college towns and redefined the campus landscape according to different values from previous decades. The bell tower, chapel, and residential buildings would represent no competition to the stadium as a landmark in the college town landscape. Football stadiums made college athletics an essential component of university life.

Fielding H. Yost and the Point-a-Minute Machine

Fielding H. Yost was one of the most influential figures in the transformation of football as a phenomenon for mass consumption in the first decades of the twentieth century. Originally from West Virginia, Yost played football at West Virginia University and led the wave in the 1890s for the first generation of full-time professional coaches. Yost had one-year contracts in Ohio, Nebraska, Kansas, Colorado, and California, where he experimented with different formations and strategies to increase team productivity. In 1900, the University of Michigan hired Yost for one year as well, in the hope of turning around a program that had lost some momentum in the Western Conferences against rivals like the University of Chicago, University of Minnesota, and University of Wisconsin.

Yost's overall strategies in Michigan created an entirely different program. Using his knowledge of young talent nationwide, Yost implemented a recruitment strategy beyond the Great Lakes region, bringing skilled players from California, Iowa, and the Eastern Seaboard to Michigan, mostly as transfer students from other programs. While regulations prohibited the immediate incorporation of transfers into varsity teams, a loophole allowed players transferring into professional schools (law, medicine, and so on) to play in their first year. Taking advantage of this loophole, new recruits from other schools gained admittance into graduate programs through the assistance and influence of Yost and the athletic department. A sophisticated network would provide new recruits with loans, university jobs, gifts, and other forms of financial subsidies to make the transfer worthwhile from a socioeconomic perspective. Yost capitalized on the information and influence provided by Michigan alumni, former Michigan athletes, and coaches around the country to identify and lure talented athletes to Ann Arbor.

Yost devised a series of offensive innovations in the field to neutralize the defensive schemes prevalent in the Western Conference that privileged weight and strength. Inspired by coaches coming from the Yale-Harvard-Princeton network, the top teams in the Western Conference fielded traditional defensive formations that focused on anticipating the coming play and closing the gap at the front line. Yost responded by recruiting fast, agile, underweight players and using a "hurry up" offensive development in which plays were called not individually but in sets, giving the defensive teams no opportunity to "read" the upcoming play and thereby reposition accordingly.[90] Lighter, faster, more agile players would participate in an offensive tempo that allowed little room for opponents to rest between plays or prepare for the next move. Yost's innovations turned the Michigan Wolverines into a light, precise, rapid machine that systematically confused and easily overcame traditional defensive formations. Rival coaches had no efficient response to such developments and frequently had to resort to illegal ways to slow down the Michigan machine-like game style through penalties and fake injuries.

For Yost, a "faster consecutive execution of the plays" would be the central element in outpacing the defensive strategies and schemes, draining the opponents' physical condition, and finally, outperforming rivals in yards and score. The hurry up system relied on speed or "rapidity," in which a set of four or five plays was called in advance. For Yost, the most important factor in the competition was not connected to height, weight, or strength; victory would always go to the faster team.

A FEW "HURRY UPS" (Fielding H. Yost).**

Hurry up.

Hurry up and be the first man to line up.

Hurry all the time; football is not a slow or lazy man's game.

Hurry up; football is a game of hurry, hurry, hurry.

Hurry up if you are behind in any play. Then is the time you need most to hurry.

Hurry up and get into every play. Football is played by eleven men. Spectators are not wanted in the field; their place is in the grand stand.

Hurry up and be the first man down the field on a punt or kick-off.

Hurry up and help your own runner with the ball; never let him go alone.

Hurry up and follow the ball. No one can play the game unless he is with the ball all the time.

Hurry up and fall on every fumble, either by your own side or an opponent. This is very important.

Hurry up and block your man hard when you should block.

Hurry up when given the ball for a gain. You must hurry or the opponents will be all over you in an instant.

Hurry up and learn the signals. You cannot play a fast game unless you know them instantly.

Hurry up and learn to control your temper. If you cannot do this you had better quit the game.

Hurry up when you are about to be tackled. Put on more "go." Don't slow up, for this is the time of all others when you need all your speed. ...

Hurry up and line up the instant the ball is dead. The delay of one man in taking his place will completely ruin fast play.

Hurry up and line up. The next play cannot start until all are ready.

Hurry up and play football. Do not slug, for slugging prevents any man from playing the team play that he should. You will be busy performing your part in the game.

Hurry up even if you are tired; do not slow down.

If you cannot stand the pace, get yourself into better condition. Football is a strenuous game.[91]

The 1901 point-a-minute Michigan team basically crushed its opponents with a new system based on speed, flexibility, and offensive creativity, producing unprecedented success in the history of the sport for the program. Students, fans, rival fans, and sports writers admired the astonishing speed developed

---

** Fielding H. Yost, Selections from *Football for Player and Spectator*. Copyright © 1905.

by Yost's Machine or the Michigan Machine. The 1901 Michigan Wolverines ended the season with an 11–0–0 record and outscored their opponents 555 points to 0, setting several records for the time, including a 128–0 victory against the University of Buffalo. Although designated third place in the nation, after Harvard and Yale, Michigan's point-a-minute machine had clearly revolutionized the offensive game in football. In 1902, Michigan broke its own record in points scored, went undefeated, and set a seemingly eternal mark for the Big Nine Conference by defeating the Iowa Hawkeyes 117–0. Yost's offensive novelties brought the most dominant offensive program in college football at the time, producing four national championships from 1901 to 1905, a 55–1–1 record, and a total score of 2,823–42. If the 1890s and the first decade of the 1900s witnessed a proliferation of Yale and Princeton football principles into the Western Conference and other programs, in the first two decades of the 1900s, Yost's hurry up gospel spread across the nation as many of his former players became foundational figures in various college programs; Vanderbilt, Oklahoma, Arkansas, Notre Dame, Purdue, Nebraska, and many others hired former Wolverine players as head coaches with the expectations of developing a program as successful as the point-a-minute machine.[92]

Yost expanded and improved the process of functional rationalization in football by incorporating speed as a systemic element in reaching a decisive competitive advantage. Following industrial processes that emphasized speed, in particular systems later envisioned as assembly lines, Yost's point-a-minute machine featured sets of consecutive plays developed on the principle of speed and precision, not power and strength.

Like Yost in Michigan, football coaches rose to regional and sometimes national prominence propelled by the combined effects of print media and radio broadcasting in the 1920s. In the 1900s, successful coaches like Walter Camp and Fielding H. Yost published contributions and books on the connections between the sports, physical fitness, and American masculinity. The next wave of coaches had a lasting and prominent presence in the print media, which covered football on a regular basis and allowed successful coaches to publish various articles on fitness and health, which were also featured on local and regional radio broadcasting. Coaches and the media crafted a very elaborate image of the college football coach as a father figure, a man maker, and a guardian of America's future. Coaches were viewed as key figures in the ideal formation of future generations of American citizens.

Mass Media and College Football

In the aftermath of the Civil War, print media increasingly dedicated more space and attention to sports events, both at collegial and professional levels.

Professional baseball, prizefighting, horse racing, and college football occupied prominent spaces in newspapers and magazines as editors realized that readership numbers would fluctuate in accordance with major sports events. The New York City-based press capitalized on sports coverage and sports sections in the last decades of the nineteenth century and prominently featured ball games, boxing bouts, and Ivy League football matches. By the turn of the twentieth century, sports coverage included stories in advance of greatly anticipated contests. "Selling the fight" pieces gained momentum in the press and would elevate the potential significance of an athletic contest with articles featuring statistics, analysis, and editorial opinion. Full coverage with "blow-by-blow" or "play-by-play" narratives constituted the central feature in event reporting. In addition, newspapers and magazines would profile "expert opinion" stories, where prominent figures in sports and sports journalism would provide their point of view on the performance of athletes and teams in a game or a season. Famous football coaches like Walter Camp, Fielding H. Yost, Knute Rockne, and many others would be regular contributors in magazines and newspapers, more often than not assisted by ghostwriters, and turn in weekly articles on sports, fitness, and health issues.

The arrival of radio broadcasting in the 1910s represented a challenge for various sports, especially because of the fear that simultaneous broadcasting of a sporting event would have a negative impact on gate revenue. Sports entrepreneurs envisioned indirect spectatorship as a direct threat to the number of fans attending the stadium. A common mistake made during this period was to equalize the number and sociodemographic profile of fans listening to a radio sports event with those who would be willing to attend the competition in person.

The arrival of electronic technologies to college sports began with the telegraph and telephone innovations in the early 1900s. In both the Ivy League and Western Conferences, student fans would follow the away performances of their teams by gathering in unions, leagues, or commons and establish a connection via telegraph or telephone with the stadium, through which they could follow the football game on a play-by-play basis. In 1912, the University of Minnesota broadcast a game via radio on 9XWLB. Nontraveling students had access to the away games by using telegraph, telephone, or radio in connection with each campus's facilities and infrastructure. In the 1920s some universities took the next step and created their own radio stations with various programming centered on football and athletics. In 1920, WTAM at College Station broadcast the Texas Agricultural and Mechanics football game in what is considered the first sports radio broadcast in intercollegiate athletics. By 1922, more than seventy universities had obtained licenses to create a radio station on campus. Commercial radio broadcasting also made significant efforts to capitalize on college football. In 1921, KDKA broadcast the Pittsburgh and West Virginia match with the sponsorship of private companies. In 1922 the Chicago vs. Princeton game was broadcast to New York City and the East Coast using telephone lines, and many of the main rivalry games began to be fully covered by radio stations, both commercial and university owned. By 1924, WGN in Chicago featured some Big Ten games, as well as Nebraska, University of Southern California, and Penn games, and from 1925 on, the Rose Bowl contest was regularly broadcast on January 1 in big city markets (Chicago, New York, Los Angeles, and so on) nationwide.[93]

Originally, technological barriers and high production costs made live broadcasting almost impossible, so events were covered in the radio station in the broadcasting booth, creating a dynamic and spontaneous interplay between the narrator and sports announcers. The announcers would reenact the game play-by-play after receiving information from the event via telegraph or telephone. This process would force the narrator to envision or imagine the full picture in each play that was just minimally described in the communication. It is no surprise that the first generations of sports radio broadcasters were accomplished storytellers with unique styles and personalities.[94]

King Football Era

The arrival of mass media to the world of college football and to some extent other college sports via newspapers, magazines, radio broadcasting, and motion pictures in the 1910s and 1920s constituted a pivotal element in the transformation of intercollegiate competitions as a national form of mass entertainment. By the 1920s, commercial radio, movie theaters, newspapers, and magazines provided extensive coverage of football before, during, and after the games.

The expansion of college football radio broadcasting came to a stop as a result of the Great Depression (1929–1933). As attendance in stadiums plummeted, university authorities looked to stop the decline by limiting and then banning radio broadcasting of college sports. In 1930, the Eastern Intercollegiate Conference prohibited football on radio altogether, and the Southern and Southwest Conferences did the same in 1932. The NCAA declared in the same year that radio was limiting football revenue but established that each program had the right to negotiate and/or ban the broadcasting of football games according to the "home rule" tradition.[95]

There was no uniform response in terms of how to deal with declining attendance rates and the impact of radio broadcasting. In 1934, for instance, the University of Michigan negotiated its football broadcasting rights with

Detroit's WWJ for $20,000. The station secured sponsorship from Chevrolet, and the transmissions went forward. In 1935, the Southern Conference reversed its policy and allowed radio broadcasting again, while the NCAA ruled in 1936 that college athletic conferences had no jurisdiction in banning their individual programs from selling broadcasting rights. For the NCAA, broadcasting rights were the property of specific universities, not conferences. Following this new format, the first televised college sports event ever was the 1939 baseball contest between Columbia and Princeton.[96]

Despite partial institutional opposition during the worst of the Great Depression, universities consolidated a radio broadcasting model based on the assistance of commercial radio corporations and, to a lesser extent, university-owned stations.

Overall, radio broadcasting of football games and other college athletics had a profound impact on American society between 1920 and 1939. The first commercial radio broadcast had a multiplying effect on the number of college football fans, as radio corporations were able to reach millions of American households, where every member of the family was a potential listener. Second, local and regional radio stations used college football to portray and display state, regional, and national rivalries and capitalize on historical, cultural, or imaginary differences. Following the format from boxing matches that exploited ethnic and national differences, radio stations presented intersectional games between Southern and Northern teams as reenactments of the Civil War, games between two local universities as family feuds, and end-of-the-season matches as championship games.

While the print media reached individual, mostly urban educated male readers, sports radio reached urban and rural populations in each state, providing them with stories about a team that represented their state against other states. College football was presented as a national sport in the sense that everybody had a team participating in the season, regardless of whether the listener had any affiliation with the college in question.

Radio broadcasting popularized college football by building on the association between football teams and each state of the nation. Between World War I and World War II, the MLB did not have a single franchise in the South, West, Northwest, or even west of the Mississippi, while every single state in the union was represented by at least one college football team. Radio also played a major role in shaping college sports as representations of American youth, spirit, and masculinity, no longer as Northeastern elite ideals, but rather as national aspirations for the general population.

Founding Fathers and Man Makers: Stagg, Rockne, and Heisman

The arrival of mass media to college sports and the consolidation of football as a form of mass spectacle in the 1920s created a new generation of head coaches with unprecedented influence in their institutions, colleges, and regions. In the 1910s, coaching football became a full professional occupation, in which the team's successful performance on the field was only one of many duties and responsibilities. Coaches performed as publicists, entrepreneurs, athletic directors, general managers, and public figures. They interacted in multiple ways with students, athletes, school authorities, politicians, business-people, alumni, and the public at large, cultivating a father-figure image that represented the institutional identity of schools and in many cases the state. As public figures, head coaches wrote, mostly through ghostwriters, many contributions in newspapers and magazines about the benefits of sports for youth, the man-building qualities of football, and the social need to supervise students and youth and channel their energy through organized sports. Following Walter Camp's example, football head coaches wrote several books on their recollections on the gridiron, their opinions on contemporary society, and their expertise of youth and organized sports. The image of the coach as a man maker cultivated by Camp in previous years became a common feature in the public persona of legendary coaches across the nation.

At the competitive level, head coaches in the 1920s led a process of hyper-specialization in functions and roles, by which they would lead a team of coaches and assistants to recruit, train, and coach their football team under the most efficient standards. Coaches would spy on rival teams while delegating their leadership to assistant coaches for tune-up games against minor rivals; recruitment would be carried through elaborate networks involving high school coaches, alumni, businesspeople, local corporations, and assistant coaches. Fitness training and nutritional regimes would expand training well into the months before and after the regular season, in order to maximize strength and neutralize competitors.

Inside universities, the role and influence of coaches underwent a considerable expansion. In many cases football coaches were also in charge of other sports and headed athletic departments, coordinating through their assistants, intramural sports, and nonvarsity football teams designed as farm teams. Institutionally, salary levels of coaches exceeded those of faculty and started to compete with the pay received by high university officials. Socially, coaches became the public face of each university, much to the chagrin of college deans and school presidents.

Figure 3.4 Amos Alonzo Stagg, University of Chicago football coach, 1906.

Amos Alonzo Stagg at the University of Chicago,[97] Fielding H. Yost at the University of Michigan, and Knute Rockne at the University of Notre Dame[98] represented the quintessential archetype of head coach as father figure. Pop Warner, Dana Bible, and John Heisman would also easily fit the standard of public patriarchs in their respective institutions in Pittsburgh, Georgia, and Texas.

Stagg started as a player for Yale in the 1880s, coached at Springfield College, and became the first hired coach at the University of Chicago in 1892. Stagg created a powerhouse from scratch to compete against the best teams, while acting as the face of the new institution (University of Chicago was established in 1890). Credited, sometimes with little evidence, with many innovations in the sport, Stagg became a legendary figure in the city of Chicago, the state of Illinois, and the world of sports. His public pronouncements and writings on the principles and benefits of Muscular Christianity for American youth cast him as an institutional father in the mass media.[99] Yost incarnated a similar character at the University of Michigan, as the primary leader in the creation of the first intramural program in the country and the brain behind the construction of the Michigan Stadium, the largest sports facility in the hemisphere.

Heisman coached Oberlin, Akron, Auburn, Georgia Tech, and Penn, among others, with significant success both on and off the field. A relentless self-promoter, Heisman had a permanent presence in regional and national media, with writings emphasizing his contributions, some more accurate than others, to football and American youth.[100]

Rockne played for Notre Dame in the 1910s and became an assistant coach in 1917 and head coach in 1919. During his tenure at Notre Dame (1918–1930), Rockne led the team to five undefeated seasons and three national championships. Like other legendary coaches of his generation, Rockne's reputation and fame was wrapped with much inaccurate or marginally factual information regarding his innovations to the game, including the forward pass.

Rockne's abilities as football coach matched his talent to propel Notre Dame football into becoming a national brand. While the small Catholic institution in Northern Indiana could barely compete in resources and fans with prestigious programs in the Ivy League or new powerhouses in the Big Ten Conference, Notre Dame was also far behind other Catholic universities in terms of enrollment and other institutional metrics. Rockne decidedly sought to attract the loyalty of Catholic fans in large urban areas (New York City, Chicago, Los Angeles, Pittsburgh, and so on) with no institutional affiliation with a particular university. Traditionally excluded and shunned by privately owned Protestant institutions, Catholic students and later Catholic communities identified with the Fighting Irish as they faced non-Catholic rivals in Yankee Stadium, Soldier Field, Los Angeles Memorial Coliseum, and other recently opened large stadiums across the country.

Figure 3.5 Notre Dame football team, 1925.

Rockne's strategy to avoid playing against other Catholic institutions[101] and to attract "subway alumni" fans in large cities turned a small program into a nationally recognized team with followers across the national territory.[102] Establishing a reliable and loyal network in urban areas with Catholic communities, Notre Dame's alumni, and Catholic high schools was crucial to Rockne's initiative. He had full-time press assistants and a regular schedule for making public speeches across the nation and writing about youth and football for newspapers and magazines. Moreover, Rockne had developed personal and professional connections with sports journalists in New York, Chicago, Detroit, and other cities, assuring continuous and positive coverage of Notre Dame football and himself in the national media. On several occasions these journalists would participate as referees in Notre Dame games, at the suggestion of Rockne.[103] Rockne's intense activities as coach, entrepreneur, general manager, writer, inspirational speaker, and father figure were abruptly interrupted in 1930, when he died in an airplane crash.

Memorializing Manly Nostalgia

Rockne's legacy at Notre Dame in 1930 was exceptional. His record as football coach (102 victories, 12 losses, and 5 ties for a .881 percentage) is still unmatched for Division I football nationwide, while few coaches (dead or alive) can compete with his five national championships. His untimely and tragic passing, en route to oversee details regarding the production of the motion picture *The Spirit of Notre Dame*, became a national tragedy, his funeral becoming a de facto head of state event.[104] The preservation of his memory became an institutional crusade at Notre Dame University, with the dedication of buildings and a statue to his name, setting a decisive trend across campuses to memorialize head coaches and players.[105]

While the elevation of Rockne's memory to the level of a deceased hero at Notre Dame University rapidly spread among alumni, Fighting Irish fans, journalists, and football fans, the production of *Knute Rockne: An All-American* in 1940, a bio-epic feature centered on the exaggerated and legendary legacy of Rockne, consecrated the reputation of the coach as a father figure for future generations.[106] Rockne the media myth replaced Rockne the historical figure, consolidating the role of the football coach as an institutional patriarch and a man maker.

Figure 3.6 Knute Rockne, 1921.

Carnegie Report and Modest Reform, 1929–1945

In the 1920s, at the sunset of the Progressive Era (1900–1929), various research institutions engaged in projects to analyze ways in which general and higher education could improve in the United States. Starting in 1906, the Carnegie Foundation commissioned the educational system from various angles.[109] In 1925 and 1927, two studies focused on the connections between athletics and schools. In 1926, the institute authorized a broad multidisciplinary research project on the links between athletics and higher education and on the impact of sports on the intellectual life of American universities in particular.[110] In 1929, the Carnegie Report entitled *American College Athletics* was released to the public.

The Carnegie Report constituted the most comprehensive social study on the history, structure, and functioning of intercollegiate athletics. A group of specialists led by Howard Savage gathered information and interviewed administrators, coaches, athletic department personnel, players, students, and alumni from 112 colleges and universities across the United States and Canada, including 18 high schools. The information analyzed covered 72 private institutions and 40 of the largest public and most prominent universities.[111]

The general report included two chapters on the history of college sports from its origins in the mid-nineteenth century to the "big-time" years in the 1920s, as well as a historical overview of the transformations of amateurism in higher education. The next chapter focused on the impact of athletics on schools and the widening gap between the social value of sports as character-building and life-preparation activities and the actual impact of interscholastic competitions on players and students.[112] The report identified a wide and pervasive culture of abuse and cheating and an overall negative impact of sports on "school boys."

The following chapters, which focused on the organization and functioning of college sports, provided a grim picture. Researchers established that the "faculty control of athletics" was a mere myth. They identified a pervasive presence and influence of interest groups with excessive power over football and athletic programs: boosters, alumni, and local businesspeople. These interest groups played a major role in the recruitment, eligibility, and academic life of players; enjoyed a special connection with coaches, athletic department heads, and school authorities; and had a decisive influence on many aspects of intercollegiate sports, from illegal assistance to players to fundraising events for large athletic infrastructure projects.

The report's conclusions in chapter 6 were unequivocal: American intercollegiate athletics were not contributing to successful undergraduate or graduate careers. Moreover, the investigators found no evidence of intercollegiate athletics making better students or better citizens. College sports had in general a negative impact on the academic life and the quality of education in the institutions analyzed. The Carnegie Report debunked the idea that athletics represented a vehicle for a successful experience in college and that organized sports benefited athletes, students, and universities as a whole.

While the construction of the largest sports infrastructure network had rested solely on the principles that athletics had a positive impact on higher education, the Carnegie Report challenged and discredited the effect of big-time football on academics altogether. Not only was there no empirical evidence of such a connection, in many ways, according to the researchers, the impact was exactly the opposite.

Chapter 7 focused on the athletes' health and identified serious issues affecting college sports participants. Each year 12 percent of varsity football players suffered a serious body injury, 25 percent suffered one or more concussions, and 16 percent of intramural football players presented similar experiences. The chapter quoted studies on the occurrence of head concussions and their severity, including a 1917 report by Edgar Fauver, who analyzed data from 374 Ivy League football players, 44 percent identified as having experienced one or more of such injuries.[113]

The Paid Coach and the Media

The second half of the Carnegie Report was dedicated to the source of the problems in intercollegiate athletics. According to the study's conclusions, the main factors responsible for the negative impact that college sports had on higher education were the paid coach and the sports media. The report did not mince words in presenting the professional coach as a major cause of the problem:

> The paid coach is at the bottom of all difficulties in American college athletics. ... Doubtless, at an ideal university professional coaching would find no place. ... A coach whose tenure depends upon victories is unfortunate and unfair ... is deleterious to sport but especially to education.[114]

In a detailed analysis, the report established the ways in which coaches violated university and NCAA rules regarding recruitment and eligibility of players. Recruitment took place via boosters, alumni, local businesspeople who used influence, money, and connections to bring athletes to universities, as well as many subterfuges to keep them there through subsidization. Athletes were persuaded to stay in their squads through economic incentives in the form of jobs, ghost jobs, money loans, scholarships, cash payments, and subsidies in kind, favors, and services. Head coaches were at the center of wide and elaborate networks in which athletes would be approached, recruited, and compensated through illegal means involving booster organizations, alumni, and local businesses.

According to the findings, 1,292 athletes reported having part-time jobs by five different employers: fraternity houses, athletic departments, boardinghouses, the university, and local businesses. In many cases the job was a "no-show" or "ghost," while others involved minimum obligations. Subsidies in cash payments, nonpayable loans, services, and favors were prevalent in private and public universities. Moreover, scholarships on academic, economic, or athletic grounds were also common features. Athletes would receive academic or economic scholarships without having to apply through the proper channels, with little to no academic requirements.

The second factor responsible for the prevalent corruption of intercollegiate athletics was, according to the report, the media. After a systematic study of several newspapers nationwide, the researchers established a positive correlation between college sports coverage and general readership in 1920s American society. Through regular precoverage of Saturday games, signature articles, and sensationalist pieces, newspapers had discovered a way to increase readership and expand the interest in college sports beyond coverage of an actual game. Likewise, the public image of college sports was framed through an exaggerated and distorted lens that elevated players to heroic dimensions and presented contests as epic battles.

After analyzing sports media in 125 newspapers from 1927, the report established that 15 percent or more of the space was dedicated to covering sports and that sports coverage had a positive impact on advertising in print media. College athletics were prevalent in newspaper advertising, especially for cars, clothing, film, and theater.[115]

In sum the Carnegie Report dissipated the long-standing association between athletics and a better academic life and education, while uncovering the existence of a parallel world in which paid coaches acted in collusion with boosters, alumni, journalists, and businesspeople to gain competitive advantages through breaking the rules. The commercialization of college sports was not incidental but an intrinsic element of the competition. The report represented the most important study on the social fabric of college athletics and its deeply rooted connections with capitalist principles for competition and organization. It also provided, from a scientific standpoint, a close view of the clear disconnect between college athletics and the principles of higher education:

> The argument that commercialism in college athletics is merely a reflection of the commercialism of modern life is specious. It is not the affair of the college or the university to reflect modern life. If the university is to be a socializing agency worthy of the name, it must endeavor to ameliorate the conditions of existence, spiritual as well as physical, and to train the men and women who shall lead the nations out of the bondage

of those conditions. To neither of these missions does commercialism
in college athletics soundly contribute.[116]

Released just at the end of the decade, and at the start of the Great
Depression, the Carnegie Report had devastating effects on the perception
of athletics by school administrators and government officials. The report's
main premise, that athletics had a negative impact on intellectual development
and academic life, represented a frontal challenge to the emerging college
sports entertainment industry. The report was widely distributed, and soon
after, the *Journal of Higher Education* summarized its findings for academics
and the general public in a separate article.[117]

Centered on the analysis of college football, the report indicated that universities could see benefits in enrollment and social visibility by engaging
in sports programs under a commercialist rationale. On the negative side,
college athletics represented a deleterious component for academic quality
and intellectual life. While criticism of college sports basically went back to
the origins of intercollegiate competitions, the Carnegie Report represented
scientific research involving every single major program and conference in
the United States.

University presidents and academic authorities responded to varying
degrees in an effort to reform college sports and reduce its commercialist aspects. While abolition of football programs was not an option for big
universities, various school authorities implemented internal regulations to
ban unethical practices in recruitment and subsidization of players. One
of the leading institutions in this initiative was the University of Chicago,
which created a strict set of rules to deemphasize the prominence of its
football program. After a series of disastrous seasons in the 1930s and a
bloody feud between university president Robert Maynard Hutchins and Amos
Alonzo Stagg, the legendary coach was dismissed in 1933. Following up with
the reformation drive, the school decided to terminate its football program
altogether in 1939 and to formally withdraw from the Big Ten Conference
in 1946.[118]

On the East Coast many institutions reacted to the Carnegie Report
in a similar way, implementing internal regulations to monitor and supervise the actions of coaches, alumni, boosters, and influential groups and
to curb the pernicious presence of commercial interests on campus. A
powerhouse program in the Northeast at NYU implemented a new policy
regarding summer training, recruitment, and subsidies standards for its
athletic department. The Violets played local games at Polo Grounds and
Yankee Stadium in the 1920s, bringing thousands of fans to the stands and
maintaining a strong team as a perennial contender to the National Championship. When the authorities decided to implement the new code, coach

John "Chick" Meehan understood competing against big programs would no longer be a viable choice, so he turned in his resignation in 1931. The outcome of football deemphasis at NYU was basically identical to the University of Chicago experience. A number of consecutive losing seasons and a sharp fall in attendance persuaded the authorities to discontinue football as a varsity sport in 1941. After a brief but failed attempt to resurrect the program in 1946, NYU chancellor decided to abolish football in 1953, citing unsustainable economic losses.[119]

Universities on the East Coast and in the Great Lakes region initiated steps to reorganize athletic departments and increase control of coaches' behavior of proselytizing and subsidizing players in their squads. Such efforts produced meager outcomes: reform efforts by presidents John Bowman (University of Pittsburgh), Thomas Gates (University of Pennsylvania), and Frank Graham (University of North Carolina) ended in failure.[120]

STUDY QUESTIONS

1. Explain the institutional responses to the "brutality and integrity" crisis in college football between 1906 and 1916.

2. Discuss the impact of new rules in college football between 1900 and 1920.

3. Discuss the differences and similarities in the financing of the construction of Harvard Stadium and Michigan Stadium.

4. Explain the impact of large steel-and-concrete stadiums on intercollegiate athletics between 1903 and 1927.

5. Explain the innovations developed by Fielding H. Yost to American football.

6. Discuss the public figure of a football coach as a man maker.

7. Discuss the Notre Dame University Fighting Irish under Knute Rockne as an example of college football for nonstudent fans.

8. Explain the elements that made Rockne an American celebrity between 1919 and 1940.

9. Discuss the methodology and main findings of the Carnegie Report.

10. Explain the negative influence of mass media on college sports, according to the Carnegie Report.

11. Discuss the role of professional coaches on college sports, according to the Carnegie Report.

12. Explain the impact of the Carnegie Report on college sports in the 1930s.

ADDITIONAL READINGS

Cooper, Jon. "Documenting the Statues on SEC Campuses and Stadiums." *Saturday Down South*. n.d. https://www.saturdaydownsouth.com/sec-football/sec-football-statues

Des Jardins, Julie. *Walter Camp: Football and the Modern Man*. New York: Oxford University Press, 2015.

Heisman, John W. "Inventions in Football." *Baseball Magazine* 1, no. 6 (October 1908): 40–42.

Kramer, Adam. 2016. "A Day in the Life of Nick Saban's Statue." *Bleacher Report*, November 11. http://thelab.bleacherreport.com/a-day-in-the-life-of-nick-sabans-statue

Kryk, John. *Stagg vs. Yost: The Birth of Cutthroat Football*. Lanham, MD: Rowman and Littlefield, 2015.

Lindquist, Sherry C.M. "Memorializing Knute Rockne at the University of Notre Dame: Collegiate Gothic Architecture and Institutional Identity." *Winterthur Portfolio* (University of Chicago) 46, no. 1 (Spring 2012): 1–24.

Smith, Ronald A., ed. *Big-Time Football at Harvard, 1905: The Diary of Coach Bill Reid*. Urbana: University of Illinois Press, 1994.

Smith, Ronald A. "Commercialized Intercollegiate Athletics and the 1903 Harvard Stadium." *New England Quarterly* 78, no. 1 (March 2005): 26–48.

Sperber, Murray. *Shake Down the Thunder: The Creation of Notre Dame Football*. Bloomington: Indiana University Press, 1993.

Treese, Joel D. 2014. "Presidents and College Football." White House Historical Association, September 24. https://www.whitehousehistory.org/presidents-and-college-football

Watterson, John S. "Political Football: Theodore Roosevelt, Woodrow Wilson and the Gridiron Reform Movement." Presidential Studies Quarterly 5, no. 3 (Summer 1995): 555–64.

Yost, Fielding H. *Football for Player and Spectator*. Ann Arbor: University Publishing Company, 1905.

FIGURE CREDITS

Figure 3.1: Source: https://commons.wikimedia.org/wiki/File:Western_Championship_Chicago_Michigan,_November_1905.jpg.

Figure 3.2: Source: https://www.loc.gov/item/2007663658/.

Figure 3.3: Source: https://commons.wikimedia.org/wiki/File%3AMichigan_Stadium_opening_3c27311.png.

Figure 3.4: Source: http://www.loc.gov/pictures/item/2001696896/.

Figure 3.5: Source: https://commons.wikimedia.org/wiki/File:Notre_Dame_football_team_1925.png.

Figure 3.6: Source: https://commons.wikimedia.org/wiki/File%3AKnute_Rockne_1921.png.

The Cold War and College Sports

A New Environment for Intercollegiate Athletics

In the aftermath of World War II (1939–1945), three different institutions played a crucial role in redefining the social position of college sports in American society: the federal government, the NCAA, and last but not least, network television. The US federal government responses to the new circumstances created by Cold War priorities played a decisive role in shaping college sports and institutions of higher education altogether. As the international competition with the Soviet Union intensified at every level, American universities in the Cold War era engaged in proactive initiatives to assist American priorities in national security, technology, economic development, international diplomacy, and elite sports.

The multiple-level competition between American and Soviet governments led to the creation of new institutions and programs to lead in the space race, technological and scientific development, military power, nuclear arsenals, economic development, education, national security, and even physical fitness, an area that became a particular source of national interest in the Eisenhower and Kennedy administrations. Having physical fitness as a national priority, private and public universities made significant efforts to participate in projects, programs, and centers focused on physical performance and sports, opening doors for the creation and proliferation of human performance and sports laboratories. Universities developed a close partnership with the federal government through grants and investments for new research agendas.[121]

Figure 4.1 John F. Kennedy in his Dexter Academy football uniform, 1926.

In the 1950s public universities led the country in developing research laboratories on human performance and sports, bringing together specialists from kinesiology, psychology, medicine, and other areas. The President's Council on Physical Fitness, for instance, was chaired by H. Harrison Clarke from the University of Oregon and had among its members professionals such as Ellsworth B. Buskirk, director of the Laboratory for Human Performance Research at Penn State University, and A.W. Hubbard, founder of the Sports Psychology Laboratory at the University of Illinois–Urbana. In 1956 Eisenhower created the Council on Youth Fitness with Executive Order 10673.[122]

Figure 4.2 Young John F. Kennedy with Harvard Swim team, 1936–1937.

The containment doctrine, which emphasized preventing the spread of communism with trade, economic development, and assistance to emerging economies around the world, led to the formation of wide initiatives with federal, state, and private funding to create programs and institutes in higher education with the mission of studying, assessing, and providing ally countries around the globe with scientific, economic, and technological assistance. Universities with area studies programs and economic development institutes proliferated.

The Soviet Union showed early leadership not only in its space program, satellite technology, and military hegemony but also in the world of international sports competitions. The Soviet challenge to US supremacy in Olympic sports started with the 1952 Helsinki Games, when the Soviet Union surprised the world by finishing second place on the medal chart.[123] Soviet athletes outperformed their rivals in several categories and obtained first place at the medal table in the 1956 Melbourne[124] and 1960 Rome Olympic Games.[125] The 1964 Tokyo Olympics final medal table presented a virtual tie, with the United States leading in gold medals and the Soviet Union in silver, bronze, and overall.[126]

The United States responded to the Soviet hegemony in athletics by restructuring the world of college athletics and by facilitating the formation of elite competitive programs around the nation, led by institutions of higher education. A revolution in college athletics expanded the number of programs, athletes, and sports to generate elite teams and individuals to face the Soviet challenge. The transformation of college athletics into the new platform for the development of elite Olympians and international athletes opened a new horizon for intercollegiate competitions beyond football and basketball, for both male and female students.

While the outside socioeconomic and political conditions changed rapidly for college athletics, the 1950s proved to be a remarkable period of internal crisis in regard to the integrity of college sports and the legal status of college athletes. The 1946 "conference of conferences" organized in Chicago by NCAA officials attempted to redefine the conditions and principles of the amateur status of athletes. Prohibition of athletic scholarships that proliferated in universities lacking the booster networks to provide economic assistance to players was at the center of the reorganization. In 1948 the NCAA approved a new code for financial aid, recruitment, academic standards, and institutional control of athletics. The main goal in the regulations was to return to the original standards of college sports, a return to "sanity"; therefore, the nickname of the "Sanity Code." Playing a more assertive role as a central institution, the NCAA assumed the authority to sanction violations and contemplated the possibility of expelling programs with severe infractions.

Enforcing the rules, however, proved to be an uphill battle for organization officials. By 1950, seven programs were found in violation of the new rules; however, none was ultimately expelled. The rule established that expulsion of delinquent programs required a two-thirds majority vote by voting members. In 1954, the NCAA created the infractions committee and a plan to certify programs nationwide. By 1956, programs received the right to present, dispute, and appeal sanctions and penalties. By 1964, the NCAA committee on infractions had become a complex organization to monitor hearings, penalties, and enforcement of rules.

Figure 4.3 Halftime show of the Orange Bowl football game, Miami Florida, 1950.

Basketball Scandals

College basketball became a popular sport for mass entertainment in the middle of the Great Depression. In 1931, Jimmy Walker, New York City mayor, commissioned a group of sportswriters to organize basketball matches in a format aimed to capitalize on rivalries between city teams and prominent outside programs; the competitions featured doubleheaders and tripleheaders with teams from New York and prestigious squads nationwide. The central goal was to secure revenue for the city relief fund. Ed "Ned" Irish, a local sportswriter, organized the basketball games following the example of the

Golden Gloves competitions in American indoor arenas. In 1934, Irish promotional games took place at Madison Square Garden, raising an unprecedented interest as mass entertainment. As Madison Square Garden began featuring college basketball on a regular basis, the popularity of the sport for the city population, most having no institutional affiliation with the competing universities, grew exponentially.

In the 1937–1938 season, these matches were presented as the National Invitational Tournament (NIT), with a marketing campaign targeted at bringing together the best programs in the nation and the victor as national champion. Despite World War II, the 1940s witnessed a steady progress for the New York–centered NIT, and Madison Square Garden became the undisputed cathedral of college basketball. Doubleheaders and tripleheaders at Madison Square Garden attracted thousands of fans from the city and beyond, while the programs rooted in the city competed against each other to get the best players from private and public high schools. As New York became the center of college basketball, local institutions like Manhattan College, New York University, City College, and Long Island University featured strong basketball squads to compete against each other and in the NIT.

The year 1950 certainly was a great one for New York City college basketball. Fans attended Madison Square Garden and other arenas by the thousands, the game was more popular than ever, and City College became the first college team to win the NIT and the NCAA national tournaments, making it the best basketball team in the nation. But 1951 could not be more of a contrast: following a long criminal investigation, New York City district attorney Frank Hogan indicted several basketball players for shaving points in exchange for monetary compensation. Hogan's indictments uncovered a wide network connecting gambling and organized crime characters with college basketball players in the city's top programs, where arrangements to manipulate the point margin were agreed on in exchange for cash payments. Charges of bribery and conspiracy against athletes created the first media scandal in college basketball history. The investigation highlighted point-shaving deals in over eighty games between 1947 and 1950, involving players from seven colleges. The most dramatic development occurred in February 1951, when the New York Police Department arrested three players from City College at Penn Station upon their return from a game in Philadelphia against Temple. The *New York Times* broke the story on February 18, 1951. While the investigation produced prison sentences for the gamblers and fixers, most players got suspended sentences, were not ultimately charged, or were acquitted. The scandal brought to light the multiple connections between gambling and college basketball and significantly tarnished the reputation of the NIT. City College, which had the highest number of players involved, was banned from playing at Madison Square Garden, and the program failed to recover in the following years.

College basketball connections with gambling and organized crime were not unique to New York City and metropolitan programs. In 1951–1952 the University of Kentucky basketball team was also implicated in a similar fashion, with an investigation uncovering point shaving and regular contacts between players and professional gamblers. The Kentucky program was suspended for an entire season in the Southeastern Conference.

Figure 4.4 Adolph Rupp, University of Kentucky men's basketball coach, 1930.

Another scandal occurred in 1951 at West Point Academy, where it was discovered that football players were involved in an academic fraud network, which provided exam information to athletes. The investigation uncovered the participation of ninety cadets in violation of the Army Cadet Honor Code. The authorities in charge decided to eradicate the problem and expelled all players involved, bringing the army's hegemony in the sport to a downhill spiral.

The early 1950s proved to be an era plagued by infractions and irregularities in the landscape of college athletics, affecting both private and public institutions. William & Mary coaches and athletes were also involved in broad academic violations. The scandal involved altered transcripts from high school and enrollment in classes that required no attendance, and it ultimately forced the resignation of football and basketball coaches, while Michigan State University and Arizona University were sanctioned for having "slush funds" to compensate players through booster networks.

Full-Time Students and Full-Time Athletes

The NCAA reaction to the 1950s scandals reshaped the policies and regulations regarding booster organizations and alumni official participation in college sports, redefined sports regulations to include legislation allowing the "death penalty" for programs with severe infractions, and finally, reinvented the legal status of college players as full-time students and full-time athletes.

The Intercollegiate Athletics Association, created in 1906 (which became the NCAA in 1910), provided the original definition of *amateurism* for college sports in unequivocal terms:

> No student shall represent a College or a University in an intercollegiate game or contest who is paid or receives, directly or indirectly, any money or financial concession or emolument as past or present compensation for, or as prior to any athletic contest, whether the said remuneration be received from, or paid by, or at the instance of any organization, committee or faculty of such College or University, or any individual whatever. ...[127]

In 1916 the NCAA redefined an amateur athlete as:

> ... one who participates in competitive physical sports only for pleasure, and the physical, mental, moral and social benefits directly derived therefrom. ...[128]

Expanding on the non-professional status of college players, the NCAA defined amateur athlete in 1922 as:

> ... one who engages in sport solely for the physical, mental or social benefits he derives therefrom, and to whom the sport is nothing more than an avocation.[129]

From the origins of the NCAA, the legal status of college players as amateur athletes became a central tenet of the organization rules and mission.

In the 1920s, college football experienced a radical transformation as a result of the building of large steel-and-concrete stadiums and the arrival of commercial radio broadcasting to the game. Numerous programs developed a sophisticated system to compensate players regardless of the NCAA rules. Athletic scholarships emerged as a common feature for the most talented players in the 1930s.

In 1948 through the Sanity Code, the NCAA adopted a new policy that recognized for the first time scholarships for athletes on the basis of academic merit or financial need and explicitly excluded athletic ability as a criterion. According to this line of thought, financial support for athletes following the regular channels of administrative scholarships was accepted, regardless of their abilities or performance in the field. Athletic scholarships, on the other hand, were definitely prohibited.

The Sanity Code generated a deep crisis in college sports, as programs refused to give up athletic scholarships or disguise them as economic need or academic merit grants. In the mid-1950s, the NCAA reconsidered the issue and formally accepted athletic scholarships for college players. Schools were permitted to offer a certain number of scholarships to athletes according to strict rules regarding eligibility, recruitment, and academic performance. The new definition of *amateurism* was now centered on an entirely new concept: student-athlete.

As athletic-based financial aid became the new standard for NCAA regulations, a national governing body delineated the rules and limits of these scholarships under the term "grant-in-aid." Athletes were entitled to receive financial support from their schools to cover tuition, fees, room and board, books, and cash for incidental expenses. This new definition of college players as student-athletes, adopted in 1956, is also the outcome of a complex history regarding the legal status of college athletes and their participation as potential laborers in institutions of higher education. Despite common stereotypes of athletes as "jocks," the history of players' activism in college sports presents numerous examples of players engaging in various forms of protest to demand better conditions. Howard University football players, for instance, decided to go on strike in 1936 before a game against Virginia Union and demanded better training and more adequate living conditions on campus, especially better food and medical assistance. Similarly, in 1937 the football team at the University of Pittsburgh demanded a $200 payment for each player to participate in the Rose Bowl. After the administration denied the request, players decided to boycott the Rose Bowl. In 1938, Pittsburgh players also organized a preseason strike, demanding athletic scholarships, collective bargaining rights, and overall better conditions. The 1937 undefeated Pittsburgh Panthers displayed a vigorous activism toward securing better conditions for the athletes. Similar cases between 1937 and 1940 involved players at Louisiana State University, the University of Nevada, and Stanford University.

A pivotal event in 1950 involved Ernest Nemeth, a football player at the University of Denver, who suffered a serious injury and demanded workers' compensation from the institution. After being rejected, Nemeth took the school to court, filing a petition with the industrial commission. The school appealed the court decision in favor of the player, and in 1953 the Colorado Supreme Court rejected the appeal and ruled on Nemeth's side. The decision set an important legal precedent in the application of the Workmen's Compensation Act to college athletics.

Soon after, a second case developed in Colorado along similar lines. The widow of Ray Dennison, a football player who died from a head injury, sued Fort Lewis A&M for death compensation benefits. While the first court ruling was on her side, the appeals court reversed it and exonerated the school from any financial liability.[130]

On October 29, 1960, the California Polytechnic football team boarded a plane to return home from a game against Bowling Green. The plane crashed, resulting in the death of Edward Gary Van Horn, one of the players. In 1963, Karen Taylor Van Horn, the widow, filed a petition in court for death benefits for her and her children. While the Industrial Commission ruled against the petition, the appeals court ruled in favor of Van Horn's widow and dependent children.

Walter Byers, NCAA executive director from 1951 to 1987, explained in detail the connections between workers' compensation complaints and the birth of the student-athlete concept:

> We crafted the term student-athlete, and soon it was embedded in all NCAA rules and interpretations as a mandate substitute for such words as players and athletes. We told college publicists to speak of "college teams" not football or basketball "clubs," a word common to the pros.
>
> I suppose none of us wanted to accept what was really happening. That was apparent in behind-the-scenes agonizing over the issue of workmen's compensation for players. I was shocked that outsiders could believe that young men on grant-in-aid playing college sports should be classified as workers.
>
> The argument, however, was compelling. In a nutshell: the performance of football and basketball players frequently paid the salaries and workmen's compensation expenses of stadium employees, field house ticket takers, and restroom attendants, but the players themselves were not covered. Even today (1995), the university's player insurance covers medical expenses for athletes, but its workmen's compensation plan provides no coverage for disabling injuries they may suffer.[131]

Despite the Nemeth and Van Horn legal victories, the NCAA implementation of the student-athlete formula consolidated the position by which the legal status of college players could not be identified as school laborers or institution workers. While the student-athlete formula institutionalized the existence of compensation to players in services, benefits, and cash, this sui generis concept also characterized the status of athletes as students and not college employees. Recent legal challenges, as exemplified by the suit initiated by Northwestern University football players in 2015, have not been successful in redefining the legal status of college players.

The NCAA and Network Television

The NCAA played a prominent role in finding an advantageous position for the creation of partnerships with network television in the 1950s. The first sporting event broadcast by television was indeed a college competition: a baseball match between Columbia and Princeton on May 17, 1939. The NBC broadcast reached four hundred television sets in New York City and was a modest success.[132]

In the 1950s, as most of the increase in the US population took place in suburban areas, television became a central element of modern life for thousands of American households. Professional sports and the entertainment industry in general suffered a substantial decrease in attendance rates, as entertainment choices in central cities became less viable options for suburban families. The NCAA scrambled in trying to protect college football from the crisis that affected the MLB, the film industry, and other downtown forms of entertainment.

While NCAA executives realized that network television was simply impossible to ignore, they attempted to find ways to limit the impact of the new medium on college stadium attendance and to protect the midsize and smaller programs from an unfair competition with prominent football programs, which would inevitably enjoy regular coverage on network television. In doing so, the NCAA became the first sports organization able to negotiate television broadcasting rights as a single package, by gaining exemption from the government to act as a monopoly. Following the traditional format from radio broadcasting, in 1950, Notre Dame and Penn signed individual broadcasting rights contracts with DuMont and ABC respectively, for the full season. The NCAA reacted by forcing both schools to withdraw from individual negotiation and lobbied to create a plan in which network television would have access to only one college football game a week, which could feature different teams according to regional coverage. In exchange, the NCAA would have an informal agreement with network television corporations not to broadcast professional football games on either Friday or Saturday. The "game of the week" format became an effective partnership between college football and commercial television, giving the NCAA a de facto status as a cartel in the establishment of broadcasting rights. From 1952 to 1981, when Oklahoma University and the University of Georgia led a legal rebellion against the limited engagement format, the NCAA successfully controlled the broadcasting rights of college sports as a single unit.[133]

Conclusions

The new circumstances created by the Cold War and the arrival of network television in college sports in the 1950s were crucial elements leading to the transformation of intercollegiate athletics and their expansion as a form of entertainment for mass consumption. College football became a remarkable example of American exceptionalism, and the NCAA effectively nurtured an image by which college football and college sports in general played a role in American culture and national priorities. The partnership and multiple interactions between college sports, the federal government, and network television produced a substantial expansion in the ways ordinary Americans perceived college football and intercollegiate athletics. The NCAA, through its maneuverings with government and the television industry, emerged in the 1950s as a different and much more powerful organization with faculties, scope, and abilities beyond those of a rules committee or an association of university presidents, as was the case in previous decades. College players were now redefined; they were no longer just students with an avocation but were student-athletes under contract by the grant-in-aid scholarships. Through their new status, they experienced a substantial transformation and became an integral part of the big-time sports and entertainment industry geared to mass consumption.

STUDY QUESTIONS

1. Describe the effects of the Cold War on intercollegiate competitions.

2. Discuss the priorities of the federal government regarding youth and fitness in the 1950s.

3. Discuss the connections between college athletics and high-performance research laboratories.

4. Explain the impact of college basketball scandals in the early 1950s on college athletics.

5. Explain the federal government policies on organized sports and inter-collegiate competitions in the 1950s.

6. Describe the transformations in the NCAA as a result of its partnerships with the television industry and the federal government.

7. Discuss the unique status of the NCAA in its ability to negotiate television broadcasting rights between 1951 and 1984.

8. Describe the premises behind the "game of the week" broadcasting format.

9. Describe how college football became a vivid example of American exceptionalism in the 1950s.

ADDITIONAL READINGS

Fit as a Fiddle. Sid Davis Productions, President's Council on Youth Fitness, LA City School District, Santa Monica Unified School District, 1961.

Byers, Walter. *Unsportsmanlike Conduct: Exploiting College Athletes*. With Charles Hammer. Ann Arbor: University of Michigan Press, 2010.

Kennedy, John F. 1961. "Remarks on the Youth Fitness Program." Adobe Flash audio, John F. Kennedy Presidential Library and Museum, July 19. https://www.jfklibrary.org/Asset-Viewer/Archives/JFKWHA-044-004.aspx.

McCallum, John D. *Big Ten Football: Since 1895*. Radnor, PA: Chilton, 1976.

McCormick, Robert A., and Amy C. McCormick. *The Myth of the Student-Athlete: The College Athlete as Employee*. 1-1-2006. Digital Commons at Michigan State University. Michigan State University College of Law.

Montez de Oca, Jeffrey. "A Cartel in the Public Interest: NCAA Broadcast Policy." *American Studies* 49, no. 3¾ (Fall/Winter 2008): 157–94.

Nelli, Humbert S. "Adolph Rupp, the Kentucky Wildcats, and the Basketball Scandal of 1951." *Register of the Kentucky Historical Society* 84, no. 1 (Winter 1986): 75–81.

Porto, Brian L. *The Supreme Court and the NCAA: The Case for Less Commercialism and More Due Process in College Sports*. Ann Arbor: University of Michigan Press, 2012.

Watterson, John Sayle. *College Football: History, Spectacle, Controversy*. Baltimore: Johns Hopkins University Press, 2000.

Wilson, Kenneth L., (Tug) and Jerry Bronfield. *The Big Ten*. Englewood Cliffs, NJ: Prentice Hall, 1967.

FIGURE CREDITS

Women and College Sports

An Uphill Battle

Women in Higher Education: Sex and Education

In 1873, the New England Women's Club invited Dr. Edward H. Clarke to speak to address the organization. The topic was *The Relation of Sex to the Education of Women*. Clarke's perspectives raised significant interest, so soon after he published a book on the subject. By 1884, *Sex and Education: A Fair Chance for Girls* had reached its fifth edition. Clarke's argument basically maintained that while women and men were equal and could reach similar goals in certain areas, they were definitely not the same and could not achieve comparable objectives by being subjected to the same educational or training processes.

> There are those who write and act as if their object were to assimilate woman as much as possible to man, by dropping all that is distinctively feminine out of her, and putting into her as large an amount of masculineness as possible. ... The loftiest ideal of humanity, rejecting all comparisons of inferiority and superiority between the sexes, demands that each shall be perfect in its kind, and not be hindered in its best work; The lily is not inferior to the rose, nor the oak superior to the clover: yet the glory of the lily is one, and the glory of the oak is another; and use of the oak is not the use of the clover. That is poor horticulture which would train them all alike.[134]

The traditional educational methods developed for male students, according to Clarke's view, would only bring disastrous results when applied to female students. A successful experience in education for women could only be made possible by taking into account the "mechanism of their bodies or blight of their vital organs." From this perspective the physical dangers that women would face in school if subjected to the same training methods as men were as serious as

> neuralgia, uterine disease, hysteria, and other derangements of the nervous system if she follows the same methods that boys are trained in. Boys must study and work in a boy's way, and girls in a girl's way. They may study the same books and attain an equal result, but should not follow the same method. ... Wherein they are men, they should be educated as men; Wherein they are women, they should be educated as women. The physiological motto is educate a man for manhood, educate a woman for womanhood, both for humanity. In this lies the hope of the race.[135]

For Clarke and his followers (in medicine, education and other areas), the participation of women in higher education necessitated the reshaping of the traditional system, which was tailored for men. The crucial modifications were to be designed to prevent serious disorders in the nervous and reproductive systems of female students. Clarke claimed that modern education and modes of modern labor had devastating effects on the mental and reproductive health of female students and workers, with negative implications for public health and national security. Moreover, he was gravely concerned that the incorporation of American women in the labor market and college life could threaten the perpetuation of a European-descent and white race majority in the population.

Clarke presented some case studies of female students attending institutions following traditional methods, highlighting the physical and mental dangers. In one study, one of his patients developed

> dyspepsia, neuralgia and dysmenorrhea, which had displaced menorrhagia. Then I learned the long story of her education and of her efforts to study just as boys do. Her attention had never been called before to the danger she had incurred while at school. She now is what is called getting better, but has the delicacy and weaknesses of American women, and, so far, is without children.[136]

According to this view, improper methods of study were at the root of many physiological disorders and ills for women in their educational life, and the increase in the number of female students and female workers could only exacerbate the gravity of this social problem:

> The number of these graduates who have been permanently disabled to a greater or less degree, or fatally injured, by these causes, is such as to excite the gravest alarm, and to demand the serious attention of the community.[137]

One of the crucial differences between male and female students was the perceived opposition between periodicity and persistence. While female students should study in "periodical tides" to reach optimal results, male students should "persist" in long time segments. The application of persistence methods to women would therefore bring about negative outcomes:

> Girls lose health, strength, blood and nerve, by a regime that ignores the periodical tides and reproductive apparatus of their organization. The mothers and instructors, the homes and schools, of our country's daughters, would profit by occasionally reading the old Levitical law. The race has not yet quite outgrown the physiology of Moses. ... Why Jane in the factory can work more steadily with the loom, than Jane in college with the dictionary; why the girl who makes the bed can safely work more steadily the whole year through, than her little mistress of sixteen who goes to school. ... For the period of the female sexual development coincides with the educational period. The same five years of life must be given to both tasks. After the function is normally established, and the apparatus made, woman can labor mentally or physically, or both, with very much greater persistence and intensity, than during the age of development.[138]

Clarke's position in favor of women attending college under a separate system and methodology encountered strong criticism from reformers in all-female colleges and coeducational universities. In 1874, Howe published a collection of essays that strongly rebutted *Sex in Education*'s plea against coeducation of female and male students in college. The passionate essays in *Sex and Education* provided empirical evidence from institutions like Oberlin College, the University of Michigan, Vassar, Antioch, Harvard, and others against the premise that college life represented a higher health risk for women than for men. In an eloquent fashion, Maria A. Elmore wrote:

> No, women may work in the factory, in the store, in the workshop, in the field, in the dining saloon, at the wash-tub, at the ironing-table, at the sewing machine,—do all these things, and many more equally hard, from Monday morning until Saturday night every week in the year; may wear their lives out toiling for their children, and doing the work for their families that their husbands ought to do, and nobody raises the arm of opposition; but just now, because there is a possibility and even probability that in matters of education women will be as honorably treated as men, lo! Doctor Clarke comes forth and tells us it ought not be so, because, forsooth, the periodical tides and reproductive apparatus of her organization will be ignored![139]

Julia Ward Howe wrote in a similar vein:

> According to him you cannot feed a woman's brain without starving her body. Brain and body are set in antagonism over against each other, and what is one organ's meat is another's poison.[140]

Caroline H. Dall also presented a rebuttal to Clarke's view on education and the sexes that emphasized, among other arguments, the differences within each group:

> For I believe the spiritual and intellectual functions of men and women to tend differently to their one end; and their development to this end, through the physical, to be best achieved by different methods. But I do not believe that any greater difference of capacity, whether physical or psychical, will be found between man and woman than is found between man and man, and my faith in the co-education of the sexes has been greatly stimulated by the present inelastic method from which many boys do shrink as much as any girl could.[141]

While the debate on coeducation continued, the consensus among progressive thinkers, college educators, and school officials was that female students needed institutional support to succeed in college without incurring health risks and potential harm in wifehood and motherhood.

A few small liberal arts colleges admitted female students in the nineteenth century: Oberlin in 1833, Guilford in 1837, Lawrence in 1847, and Antioch in 1853. A pivotal change came about as Northeastern elite institutions sponsored the formation of "sister" institutions for female students from elite families. This major development contemplated the offering of courses in most of the same disciplines as for male students, not merely the teaching, nursing, and homemaking choices available to women in other colleges. Between 1837 and 1889 Ivy League's Seven Sisters (Barnard College, Bryn Mawr College, Mount Holyoke College, Radcliffe College, Smith College, Vassar College, and Wellesley College) led the nation in offering college degrees to women with classes and requirements similar to those provided to male students at Harvard, Columbia, or Princeton.

In the aftermath of the Civil War the participation of women in higher education increased significantly. Traditional colleges for women expanded their enrollment while new institutions opened their doors to female students. Moreover, the curricular choices for female students outgrew the traditional paths associated with domestic labor or an extension of motherhood roles. Women participated in careers no longer limited to nursing, teaching primary school and the like. Following the lead by elite private institutions in the Northeast, various colleges for women offered curricular content very similar to what was offered at men's universities.

Public universities also opened their doors to female students while maintaining a predominantly male student population. The new horizons for American women in college were a parallel development with substantial increases in the participation of women in the labor market, politics, culture, and entertainment in the Gilded Age.

While progressive ideologies welcomed such new developments, a counter current presented vigorous objections to the participation of women altogether in public arenas and social spaces previously occupied by all-male populations.

Clarke's views must be considered in the background of such debates in which conservative groups challenged the new places to which women were gaining access, progressive groups demanded unrestricted and equal access, and moderate groups attempted to reach a position of compromise, with women gaining some access under modified conditions fit for traditional views on the female body and subordinated position.

The participation of women in college sports departed, therefore, from historical circumstances affecting male students in the same period. In light of the fact that athletes represented their institutions through their participation in public sports activities, the display of female athleticism certainly was at the center of debates concerning the potential dangers of women attending college or playing by rules designed for male students according to tradition and custom.

On the one hand, the moderate view became a central tenet of the reformers' view on women in college and more specifically, women in college sports. On the other hand, the participation of women in college sports would only exacerbate and expand the controversies about the potential negative effects of college life, and more specifically, college athletics on the female students' bodies.

In Loco Parentis and Muscular Christianity

Since the origins of university life in the United States, continuing well into the 1950s and 1960s, authorities and officials in institutions of higher education invoked the in loco parentis legal principles to establish, regulate, and supervise the boundaries of acceptable behavior for students inside and especially outside the classroom. Universities had the right and responsibility to prescribe and protect the good manners and moral behavior of the student population residing on campus and attending classes.

Extracurricular activities, clubs, Greek life, gastronomic societies, and poetry gatherings could be part of student life and the outcome of student initiatives, but the institution or alma mater had the ultimate decision as to whether such activities constituted normal or unbecoming behavior. In loco parentis (in place of parents), therefore, provided colleges and universities with the legal standing to regulate student life and act as moral guardian.

In the nineteenth century colleges only sporadically and reluctantly looked for ways to regulate sports for male students. While faculty and authorities considered these activities of little value in the educational arena, they hesitated to curb, regulate, or prohibit them except for only a few instances. Football was prohibited at Harvard, Yale, and other institutions at various points, only to be reimplemented in a short time. Institutions tolerated sports for male students as an escape valve in order to prevent social unrest and rioting on campus.

The situation in institutions for female students was diametrically opposed, since the ideal qualities projected in intercollegiate competitions (strength, determination, character, aggressiveness, persistence, endurance, and so on) were generally associated with masculine identities. As was the case with their male counterparts, female students organized athletic competitions, along with many other social activities, for recreational purposes on campus to articulate a leisure life and to create social bonds. Between 1850 and 1870 women students on the Northeastern Seaboard and other areas participated in sports activities like baseball, track and field, rowing, and others. Perceived by the student population as the ideal outlet for sporting communities that proliferated on campus, such events and competitions took place in public spaces and raised concern, and in some cases outrage, by college authorities and administrators.

The Progressive Era

At the dawn of the twentieth century, a wide movement for equal rights for women generated significant changes in the participation of female students in university life and college athletics. Dissatisfied with the traditional precepts that discouraged women from participating in sports, a new generation of physical educators, teachers, and school officials embraced the benefits of organized sports for girls and young women in the educational system.

Girls and women in American society participated in physical activities, recreational outings, and organized sports more than ever before in the history of the country. Access to recreational areas, a progressive goal since the 1850s, proliferated in urban enclaves.

In the 1850s Central Park in New York City became the classic model of a pastoral space for urban classes, as seen in Brooklyn, Philadelphia, Boston, and Chicago. Many other American cities throughout the country followed this example by creating outdoor social spaces where people could participate in leisure activities. Progressive Americans in the early twentieth century redefined parks as spaces for active recreation and focused on more organized physical activity. The playground movement, centered on the idea that public spaces should be safe, open, and accessible to youth and families, created new venues for physical activities in recreational areas. Field houses, sports fields, bicycle and walking paths, and playgrounds became defining elements in the progressive park model. Park commissions in large cities developed full programming activities, making sports available to boys and girls as part of their recreational amusement.

Women's colleges expanded their physical education curricula and the participation of female students in athletic events mostly through the formation of clubs and sporadically though intercollegiate competitions. The progressive movement generated new interest in developing sports for women in schools and colleges. While the general opinion among reformers clearly discouraged the participation of female students in sports, a new generation of progressive educators engaged in new ways to provide physical education using sports and organized competitions.

Smith College Archives

Figure 5.1 Senda Berenson holding the ball in women's basketball, 1903.

In 1899, Senda Berenson, a physical education director at Smith College, established basketball activities and games for the students. Berenson modified the game rules in order to make them more moderate and more in line with physical education goals and less associated with "masculine" attributes, such as strength, aggressiveness, and physical contact. According to her rules, players were not allowed to steal or "snatch" the ball, points were deducted for fouling, the court was divided in three equal segments, and players were assigned to each segment without the chance to participate in any of the other two. Dribbling was also prohibited; players could bounce the ball no more than three times before passing it to a teammate.

The principles of modification and moderation in women's sports at Smith College soon became the norm for female students in college as well as high school. Berenson's redesigned rules for women's basketball became the official rules for basketball competitions in scholastic and college events.

In 1903 Berenson published *Basket Ball for Women*, with additional articles by medical and college authorities praising the adaptation of the game to fit the moderate principles of physical education for women. Basketball in the Berenson Rules format presented multiple psychological and physiological benefits; it was practical and represented a more advanced and entertaining form of the game for physical education programs. Authorities from Radcliffe College, the University of Michigan, the Boston Normal School of Gymnastics, and others endorsed the rules.[142] The Berenson Rules became a model for adapting other sports for women athletes: boxing, football, wrestling, rugby, and water polo.

Progressive reformers considered moderate sports ideal for female students and American girls in general but shared the same opinion as traditional medical and religious authorities in regard to the dangers that manly sports presented for the nervous and reproductive systems of the female body. In this context moderated sports and organized physical activities for girls proliferated outside the boundaries of country clubs and athletic clubs and extended into urban playgrounds, school grounds, high school classes and tournaments, city leagues, and college classes and competitions.

From the reformers' perspective, no-contact sports like tennis, golf, swimming, track and field, and gymnastics were at the top of the list of acceptable developing activities for girls, while moderate and modified sports like basketball, softball, volleyball, and soccer were encouraged but only under strict supervision. "Manly" sports such as football, wrestling, and boxing were absolutely not tolerated.

Within the boundaries of such ideological values, reformers in the Progressive Era became the sponsors of women's sports in city leagues, public schools, state championships, Y-women centers, and intercollegiate athletics. Although initially the focus was certainly placed on the benefits that moderate exercise represented for the success of female students and urban residents in the modern era, the incorporation of female athletes in competitive events had become an irreversible trend prior to World War I (1914–1918).

The Roaring Twenties

As the United States became a world power in the aftermath of World War I, a second wave in the history of women and sports generated transformational changes in the nature and social status of the competitions featuring female Olympian and college athletes. State basketball championships for women captured considerable attention from the media and sports clubs. Varsity sports proliferated in women and coed colleges, female American tennis stars represented their country in international matches, and female Olympians gained national attention winning medals in most events. At the higher education level, national meetings for women athletes in swimming, track and field, and other sports gained considerable momentum and became regular features in the institutional programming of their colleges and universities. Working women participated in industrial leagues and city tournaments and few explored the possibilities of joining traveling teams, playing in men's leagues, and reaching into the area of semiprofessional and professional sports.

Figure 5.2 Sybil Bauer, 1922.

Sybil Bauer exemplifies the trajectories of this new generation of female athletes. Born in Chicago in 1903 to a Norwegian family, Bauer entered the world of swimming through the city interscholastic system and became a student at Northwestern University, where she also played basketball and field hockey. Bauer's swimming performances gained her local recognition, setting new records in more than twenty races. In 1922, Bauer broke the men's backstroke record, a feat she repeated two years later. In 1924, she represented the United States in the Olympic Games in Paris, earning the gold medal in backstroke. Bauer petitioned to participate in the men's race, but her request was denied.

Bauer's trajectory from Chicago to the Olympic Games enjoyed ample coverage from mass media and represented an example of the multiple benefits reformers saw in the participation of girls in moderate athletics.

In a similar path, Gertrude Ederle became a media star when she became the first woman to swim across the English Channel. A product of New York City public pools, Ederle grew up participating in various swimming competitions. Crossing the tempestuous waters between northern France and southern England in fourteen hours and thirty-one minutes represented a first for women in athletics, not to mention a world record for all swimmers that remained unbeaten until 1950.

Born in 1905 in Centerville, California, and a student from the University of California–Berkeley, Helen Wills was an eight-time Wimbledon champion, a record that remained unbroken until the 1990s. The first female sports superstar with her face on the cover of *Time* magazine (in 1926 and 1929), Wills won two Olympic gold medals in the 1924 games in Paris, which brought her media celebrity. Wills refused to play in the traditional long-dress etiquette for women in tennis and chose to wear a short skirt and tight clothes instead, in order to enhance speed and movement. Her performances inspired youth across the country to become tennis players.

American women made substantial progress in the sports arena as a result of the strong emphasis progressive reformers placed on universal education, access to public schools at no cost, and the expansion of public facilities to practice sports in urban areas. In the context of the suffrage movement and the wide social activism in favor of equal rights for women, the participation of women in sports became a crucial public space to challenge traditional prejudice and conventional chauvinism.

Prominent women athletes in the 1920s became the first generation to enjoy significant coverage by mass media and to reach celebrity status as independent and powerful symbols of America's new international status. Bauer, Ederle, Wills, and others received substantial attention in film newsreels, newspapers, magazines, and radio broadcasting, although the feature stories, written by male journalists, emphasized the athletes' "feminine beauty" and commitment to traditional gender roles.

While athletes like Wills and Bauer became icons of American national identity for their achievements in international arenas, their institutional affiliation with Berkeley and Northwestern was not an angle developed in the mass media coverage. Both were rarely seen as college stars or symbols of their alma mater. Institutional identification associating universities with female athletes was notably absent in the regular features of the mass media.

Women in Higher Education: Sex and Education

In the 1920s, college sports for women had expanded beyond the boundaries of clubs, physical education programs, and campus leisure activities but remained definitely subordinated to male athletics sponsored by the same institutions. Basketball, track and field, swimming, and other moderate, noncontact sports for women became competitive under newly formed organizations like the Amateur Athletic Union (AAU). Completely excluded by the NCAA, definitely trivialized by mass media, and certainly relegated to a discreet existence by colleges and universities, women's intercollegiate sports remained a clear example of the differential experiences of men and women in institutions of higher education and society in general.

Moreover, the expansion of physical education, interscholastic competitions, and industrial and recreational leagues produced a substantial increase in the participation of girls and women in organized sports. New generations of women writers coming from medicine, physical education, and sociology produced studies on the educational, physiological, and social benefits of organized sports for American women in general.

Clelia D. Mosher published *Personal Hygiene for Women* (1927), Florence A. Somers *Principles of Women's Athletics* (1930), and Agnes R. Wayman *Education through Physical Education* (1928). The expansion in girls practicing sports was also reflected in numerous pamphlets and monographs on how to teach and organize sports for women and the positive outcomes from such activities. In New York City, A.S. Barnes and Company published the *Athletics for Women Series*, which featured specialized works on baseball, basketball, tennis, gymnastics, track and field, volleyball, field hockey, and even "Tumbling, Pyramid Building and Stunts."[143]

WWII and the Cold War

Despite the massive participation of American women in the national economy and the substantial increase of female students in college during World

War II, college sports remained a hypermasculine space in the 1940s and the following decades. The Cold War era did not bring about any considerable transformation. With the exception of few programs across the nation looking to groom high-performance female athletes for Olympic competitions, college sports remained an almost exclusive domain for male athletes and students.

Institutional support for female athletes was practically nonexistent, and most of the sports activities for women were confined to physical education routines and club-status teams with sporadic competitions and recreational games.

> Before the passage of Title IX in 1972, only 32,000 women per year played college sports. Athletic scholarships for women were virtually non-existent, and many colleges had no women's sports programs at all. At the high school level fewer than 300,000 girls competed in sports each year, representing only 7% of interscholastic athletes nationwide. Girls who did play sports in high school received dramatically different treatment in equipment, coaching, practice times, and sports offerings.[144]

Most institutions in higher education offered little or no support to female athletes beyond the context of physical education and recreational clubs. While outdoor activities were seen as positive for students, such as hiking, canoeing, and camping, administrators rarely encouraged female students to participate in intercollegiate competitions. Clubs functioned on voluntary basis, with a sports manager who would be informally in charge of organizing outings and games. Competitions were reduced to interclass events and events where the demonstration of skills would be emphasized. Intramural athletics for women were merely a minor element of social life, where volunteerism compensated for the lack of institutional support. Women athletes could and did organize "acceptable" team sports (volleyball, soccer, softball, field hockey, and so on) and participated in them as extracurricular activities. Student and local newspapers rarely covered these women sports beyond the pervasive sexualization of the female body. Athletic departments also ignored these events. In order to research such clubs and competitions, historians have had to examine yearbooks and promotional pamphlets, the only outlets that provided information about club life for women on campus.

The history of the Green Splash club at Michigan State University illustrates the experiences of women in sports in public universities. Starting in the early 1920s as the Women's Life Saving Corps, aimed at teaching swimming and water survival skills to female students, the group became the Green Splash in 1927.[145] In the 1950s, the Green Splash featured synchronized swimming events and an annual water show with elaborate choreography and set designs. While members of the club also competed on AAU and Big Ten swimming meets, the emphasis of the organization was on providing skilled demonstration performances for the entertainment of students and the general public. Annual water performances followed specific themes each year ("The Greatest Splash on Earth" in 1954 and "Sounds of Music" in 1966), and swimmers or "synchronettes" would wear extravagant costumes, facial makeup, and elaborate hairdos.[46] The Green Splash also organized presentations as opening acts or sideshows to swimming and diving competitions and provided clinics for high school girls to start their own aquatic teams. The display of "femininity" and theatrical features was presented in contrast to the strength and "masculine" attributes of the male swimmers and athletes.

Figure 5.3 Ohio State's first female cheerleading squad, 1938.

In the 1950s, cheerleading became an institutionally supported option for women willing to participate in public physical activities under the restrictions of college life. Sponsored by athletic departments and school officials, cheerleading transitioned from being an all-male social ritual to becoming a predominantly female activity. Cheerleading rapidly evolved as a performance to reassert the central role of male sports and the supportive secondary role of women. In this subordinated relationship, college and high school cheerleaders performed as a sideshow to football and other male sports where they showcased female characteristics—supportiveness, enthusiasm, and sexual attractiveness—as auxiliary complements to the public hegemonic masculinity embodied by the male athletes.[147] In the 1950s, state school officials encouraged cheerleading and beauty contests in North Carolina yet discouraged competitive sports for women, particularly basketball.[148]

According to Pamela Grundy:

> The triumph of cheerleading over both varsity sports and physical education underscored the growing risks inherent in the strategy physical educators had adopted when they turned their backs on varsity athletics in favor of more privately focused character-building efforts. In their campaign against varsity sports, North Carolina's physical educators had set themselves a bold and ambitious task. Rather than meshing their athletic philosophy with the society taking shape around them, they sought to fashion games and sports that challenged some of the baseline assumptions of twentieth-century society—the significance of competition, financial success, popularity, and feminine appearance.[149]

Title IX Era

The civil rights movement consolidated some of its gains with the passing of the Civil Rights Act of 1964 which prohibited discrimination in education, employment, and public accommodations on the basis of race, nationality, religion, and gender. Moreover, the Civil Rights Act eliminated tax polls and literacy requirements for participating in elections at local, state, and national levels. Richard M. Nixon signed Title IX legislation of the Education Amendments (1972) during his second term of presidency.[150]

> Title IX Era
> ... Section 1681.
> Sex Prohibition against discrimination; exceptions.
>
> *No person in the United States shall, on the basis of sex, be excluded from participation in, be denied the benefits of, or be subjected to discrimination under any education program or activity receiving Federal financial assistance.*[151]

Overall, Title IX is responsible for the massive incorporation of female students in varsity sports between 1970 and 2000. Right before the amendment, fewer than 15 percent of female athletes participated in varsity sports, while by 2001 the percentage of women in competitive sports in higher education reached 45 percent.

The pace of the change deserves its own explanation, since various institutions participated actively, and on opposite sides, in the interpretation and implementation of Title IX. During the 1970s, a common interpretation of the amendment in higher education was that it did not cover nor include athletics.

The NCAA, most college football coaches, and most athletic department directors clearly opposed the instrumentation of Title IX regulations. Arguing that athletics was not mentioned in the original legislation, most prominent administrators sided with the opposition against including sports in the initiative for gender equity in education.

Figure 5.4 Senator Birch Bayh with Title IX athletes, Purdue University, ca. 1970s.

As early as 1974, Senator John Tower proposed an amendment to exempt athletics altogether from the Education Amendment. The "Tower Amendment" failed to pass, but it inspired Senator Jacob Javits to propose an exemption of sports with large crowds, namely football and basketball. A similar attempt to exempt revenue sports proposed in 1975 by Representative James G. O'Hara also failed to pass.[152] In 1976, the NCAA challenged the legality of Title IX after several failed attempts to exempt revenue sports through other means.[153]

Despite such efforts, Title IX was officially passed in 1977, and in 1979 the US Department of Education made an explicit mention of athletics and published its policy interpretation guidelines for intercollegiate athletics; however, the investigator's manual was not issued by the Office of Civil Rights until 1990.[154]

The reason for this lapse resides in the legal challenges to the inclusion of athletics on Title IX by various parties in the 1980s. A crucial outcome came about in the *Grove City College v. Bell* decision, when the Supreme Court ruled that Title IX legislation only applied to particular programs that directly benefited from federal funds and that athletic departments with no contributions from the federal government were consequently not obligated to enforce the legislation.[155]

The legal debate continued and was finally resolved in 1987–1988 with the passing of the Civil Rights Restoration Act, which established that institutions receiving federal funds must comply with Title IX and all other civil rights laws in all instances, whether or not specific programs or departments directly benefit from federal resources. President Ronald Reagan vetoed the act, but in 1988 the veto was overridden by the US Congress. The Civil Rights Restoration Act was finally enacted on March 22, 1988.[156]

Figure 5.5 Louisiana Tech women's basketball team, 1982.

In 1988, female athletes at Temple University took legal action to demand equality in athletics for both sexes, arguing that the school had displayed substantial discriminatory practices in resources allocated to programs, financial aid for female athletes, and participation of women students in athletics. The case was settled within a few months and set a remarkable precedent on ways to demonstrate gross disparities in the treatment of men and women in athletics. The *Haffer v. Temple* decision became a landmark for sex discrimination in athletics nationwide.[157]

In 1992 *Franklin v. Gwinnett Public Schools* involved a high school student who had been continuously victimized by her teacher/sports coach with sexual harassment. The petitioner claim demanded damages under the 1972 Title IX statutes, setting a precedent for Title IX legislation and sexual abuse in higher education. The Supreme Court ruled that victims of sexual abuse were entitled to monetary damages under Title IX legislation.[158]

To further monitor and advance the implementation of gender equity in athletics and its transparency, in 1994, the US Congress passed the Equity in Athletics Disclosure Act, which made mandatory for institutions the public disclosure of gender participation statistics and budgetary expenses in college athletics. From that point on, colleges and universities were required to release updated information on the ways in which their athletic programs are in process to comply with gender equity in their varsity teams.[159]

As the actions of school officials and athletic directors became available to public scrutiny, the participation of female athletes proved to be a crucial element in the struggle for gender equity in sports. Athletes around many campuses engaged in social activism and legal action to activate the instrumentation of Title IX regulations and standards. In 1991, Brown University demoted women's gymnastics and volleyball teams from varsity status. Athletes initiated a class action suit against the administration to reinstate the teams as varsity squads. In 1996, the courts ruled that the school had engaged in gender discriminatory practices and ordered the reinstatement of the teams.[160] Through the 1990s, major court decisions sided with plaintiffs for violations of Title IX legislation. Female student athletes at Colorado State, Indiana University, and Colgate University earned favorable rulings forcing their institutions to change old ways.[161] In similar developments university administrators at the University of Texas–Austin and the Virginia Polytechnic Institute, facing Title IX violations in court, reached settlements to increase the institutional commitment to gender equity in college sports.[162] In 2007, former associate athletics director Diane Milutinovich won a gender discrimination legal dispute against Fresno State and was awarded a $3.5 million settlement, expanding Title IX application to include the rights of female employees in athletic departments.[163]

Title IX legislation implementation is monitored according to a three-prong test standard: substantial proportionality, history and continuing practice, and effective accommodation of interests and abilities. According to legal scholars Deborah Brake and Elizabeth Caitlin:

> Under the first prong, the court examines whether athletic participation opportunities are provided to each sex in numbers substantially proportionate to their enrollment. If a school cannot meet this prong, the court then determines whether the school can demonstrate a history and continuing practice of program expansion for the underrepresented sex. If a school fails the second prong, the court finally asks whether the athletic interests and abilities of the underrepresented sex have been fully and effectively accommodated by the school. If the plaintiffs can show that the school also fails on this third prong, then the court must find the

school out of compliance with Title IX. In applying this three-prong test, courts have arrived at the same conclusion: that the schools that have been challenged to date have failed to provide adequate opportunity to their female athletes and thereby are violating federal law.[164]

Current legislation on the Title IX Education Amendment stipulates that discrimination on the basis of gender is prohibited in any interscholastic, inter-collegiate club or intramural athletics. It also indicates that equal opportunity provisions for both sexes must include

> the provision of equipment, scheduling of games and practice time, travel and per diem allowances, assignment and compensation of coaches, provision of locker rooms, provision of medical and training facilities, provision of housing and dining facilities and publicity.[165]

In the 2010s, the Department of Education made explicit that the Title IX legislation established protections against sexual harassment and sexual violence, and that such protections are extended to all students, athletes and otherwise. Along with it, the agency opened investigations on the subject on several campuses, established guidelines to prevent and react to sexual violence, and embraced a proactive policy to monitor complaints involving student athletes.[166] The Department of Education Office of Civil Rights has opened several investigations into the handling of sexual assault cases by institutions of higher education and their responses to sexual harassment cases. While the official number has not been disclosed, according to some sources, between 2012 and 2016, there were 246 cases of sexual violence involving 195 institutions.[167]

The overall impact of Title IX legislation on intercollegiate athletics has been the expansion of the participation of women in varsity sports, the increasing visibility of women's athletics, and the substantial progress toward more equal treatment of women in intramural, club, and varsity sports. While the amendment became public law in 1977, the implementation of the regula-tions entered an accelerated process only in the 1990s. By the early 2000s, almost three decades after the passing of the amendment, Title IX policies had definitely changed the landscape of college athletics. In the 2000–2001 academic year, women made up 55 percent of the student population and 42 percent of varsity athletes.[168]

While practically no school has reached a distribution of varsity athletes that closely reflects the gender balance of the student population, in the 1990s, athletic departments finally initiated a systematic drive to incorporate more women into varsity sports and to provide comparable treatment in equipment, facilities, coaching, training, and scheduling.

The NCAA, after presenting fierce opposition to the legality and instrumentation of Title IX in the early years, reversed its position and embraced the principles of gender equity in college sports. Starting in the 1981–1982 school year, the NCAA organized national championship competitions for women in twelve sports, with North Carolina winning the first NCAA women's basketball championship. Currently, the NCAA organizes national tournaments in twenty-four sports, most for both sexes, with the exceptions of football and wrestling. Female athletes now participate in varsity sports traditionally perceived as "masculine," like ice hockey or water polo.[169]

Contrary to common misperceptions about the impact of quotas on college athletics and the connections between gender equity and male varsity teams, recent studies by Anderson-Cheslock and Ehrenberg show that, between 1995 and 2000, the overall number of varsity teams and varsity athletes increased for both men and women. While in some instances athletic departments have attempted to reach gender proportionality in their teams by discontinuing non-revenue male varsity squads, the study demonstrates that the general impact of Title IX has been positive for both male and female student-athletes.[170]

A new and maybe more courageous challenge for the Title IX amendment would be the substantial decrease and eradication of sexual harassment and sexual violence across colleges and universities in the United States, a goal in full alignment with the end of sexual discrimination in education.

STUDY QUESTIONS

1. Discuss the arguments against the participation of women in higher education in the late nineteenth century.

2. Describe the reaction by school authorities to the formation of sporting communities by female students in the nineteenth century.

3. Explain the role of Muscular Christianity and in loco parentis principles in the marginalization of women in college sports.

4. Explain the values of the Progressive Era (1900–1929) that shaped the participation of women in school and college sports.

5. Describe the new developments for female college athletes in the 1920s.

6. Explain the proliferation of cheerleading squads in the 1940s and 1950s.

7. Discuss the initial impact of Title IX in the 1970s.

8. Describe the legal battles to neutralize the implementation of Title IX before 1990.

9. Discuss the various strategies female athletes engaged in to reach equity in college sports as stipulated by Title IX legislation.

10. Explain the overall impact of Title IX for male and female athletes.

ADDITIONAL READINGS

Berenson, Senda, ed. *Basket Ball for Women*. New York: American Sports, 1903.

Brake, Deborah, and Elizabeth Caitlin. "The Path of Most Resistance: The Long Road toward Gender Equity in Intercollegiate Athletics." *Duke Journal of Gender Law & Policy* 3, no. 51 (1996): 51–92.

Cahn, Susan K. *Coming on Strong: Gender and Sexuality in Twentieth-Century Women's Sport*. Cambridge, MA: Harvard University Press, 2003.

Clarke, Edward H. *Sex in Education: A Fair Chance for Girls*. Boston: Houghton, Mifflin, 1884.

Grindstaff, Laura, and Emily West. "Cheerleading and the Gendered Politics of Sport." *Social Problems* 53, no. 4 (November 2006): 500–18.

Howe, Julia Ward. *Sex and Education: A Reply to Dr. E.H. Clark's Sex in Education*. Boston: Robert Brothers, 1874.

Mosher, Clelia D. *Personal Hygiene for Women*. Stanford, CA: Stanford University Press, 1927.

Smith-Rosenberg, Carroll, and Charles Rosenberg. *From 'Fair Sex' to Feminism: Sport and the Socialization of Women in the Industrial and Post-Industrial Era*. Abingdon, UK: Routledge, 1987.

Somers, Florence A. *The Principles of Women's Athletics*. New York: Barne, 1930.

FIGURE CAPTIONS

Figure 5.1: Katherine E. McClellan, "Senda Berenson holding the ball in women's basketball, 1903," Smith College Archives. Copyright © 1903.

Figure 5.2: Source: https://commons.wikimedia.org/wiki/File:Sybil_Bauer.jpg.

Figure 5.3: "Ohio State's first female cheerleading squad, 1938," The Ohio State Library/Archives.. Copyright © 1938.

Figure 5.4: Source: https://commons.wikimedia.org/wiki/File%3ABirchWorkout.jpg.

Figure 5.5: Copyright © Anonymous (CC BY-SA 3.0) at https://commons.wikimedia.org/wiki/File:1982_Louisiana_Tech_women%27s_basketball_team.jpg.

6

College Sports and African Americans

Introduction

This chapter provides a historical overview of the participation of nonwhite athletes in college sports before, during, and after the civil rights movement, placing a special emphasis on the struggles to participate on equal terms on and off the field. It presents the historical transformations of racial segregation in college sports and provides a detailed account of the different periods in the American quest for equity in athletic competitions.

Intercollegiate sports from their inception in the nineteenth century have been a social space that mirrors and reproduces the general social dynamics sustaining racial hierarchies and patriarchal values. Contrary to common perceptions about colleges and universities as places exempted from prejudice and biases prevalent in the general society, institutions of higher education have consistently displayed patterns that reflect and reinforce the subordinated structures in which dominant groups have established norms to enhance racial and gender inequities.

Segregated Integration Era, 1890–1945

Despite the promising developments at the end of the nineteenth century, college football teams in the Big Ten and the Midwest displayed a consistent resistance to integrate African American athletes on a regular basis. George Jewett, Fred Patterson, Preston Eagleson, and others constituted sporadic examples in which teams had room for only one athlete of color at a time. Jewett played for the University of Michigan and Northwestern University in the 1890s, while Patterson joined the Ohio State football team in 1891. George

A. Flippin played for the University of Nebraska in 1891, and Eagleson joined the Indiana football squad in 1893. Bobby Marshall played for Minnesota from 1904 to 1906. In the first decades of the twentieth century, as college football became entertainment for mass consumption, integrated teams rarely ventured beyond these institutional boundaries. Michigan Agriculture College, for instance, included a black player for the first time in 1912. Born in Virginia, Gideon Smith played three seasons as tackle and later joined the Canton Bulldogs in the professional ranks. For the following decades, Michigan Agriculture College football remained an all-white program.

While public universities outside Southern states had no legal impediments to include black and other nonwhite athletes, in reality they had structured an informal segregation system, enforced by coaches and athletic directors, in which each team would admit one player of color on an irregular basis. Such a "gentlemen's agreement" was the basic rule for college football well before the arrival of the intersectional games in the 1920s and 1930s between Southern universities and their Northern and Western counterparts.

Black Colleges and University Sports

Since education was segregated by law in Southern states at all levels, the participation of African American athletes was institutionally prohibited in Southern universities and, consequently, confined to the world of black colleges and universities, which were constantly struggling for resources and support. In such a limited sphere, black teams would only play against one another rarely. The first documented college football match between Livingston and Biddle University (later Johnson C. Smith) took place in North Carolina on December 27, 1892.[171]

During the Progressive Era (1900–1929), public education outgrew and surpassed the traditional model in higher education. Public high schools surpassed private preparatory schools and public state-funded universities, and normal schools experienced a substantial demographic expansion. The number of participants in school athletics also underwent a dramatic increase. While the common perspective by school coaches and physical educators was that physical education and sports should be offered to the entire student population, their take on competitive collegiate sports was very similar to the perspective in private elite schools in regard to integration, and therefore public institutions rarely included nonwhite athletes in their competitive team sports. In the 1910s, as public universities experienced a substantial growth, new opportunities opened for African American students in college sports, especially in track and field.

The first was Howard P. Drew who became national A.A.U. champion at 100 yards in 1912 and 1913 while at Springfield (Mass.) High School. In 1913 he also won the 220-yard title. In 1914 Drew went to the University of Southern California where he became co-holder with Arthur Duffey of Georgetown of the world's record of 9.6 seconds for the 100-yard dash, a mark which stood for many years. Drew also equalled the world's record for the 220-yard sprint when that was 21.2 seconds.[72]

The successes of Drew and Duffey in Springfield and Southern California inspired other schools to allow black athletes in their track and field squads. By the 1920s, the sport included stars like DeHart Hubbard at the University of Michigan, Sol Butler at Dubuque, and later, Ed Gordon at the University of Iowa.

The 1920s witnessed a proliferation of inclusive track and field teams where African American athletes began to dominate across conference, national and Olympic competitions. The University of California–Los Angeles, University of Chicago, NYU, University of Michigan, and Syracuse University, among others, featured black athletes in many events.

By the 1930s, African American sprinters like Eddie Nolan, Ralph Metcalfe, and Ed Gordon dominated in 100-meter, 200-meter, and long jump college and Olympic events. The University of Michigan continued its policy of including black sprinters with Willis Ward, while other schools adopted the same principles. Illinois State had James Johnson, Ohio State Jesse Owens, and the University of Pittsburgh Everett Utterbach.[73]

Race and Athletics: Elmer Mitchell's Views

Within the confines and restrictions of the integrated segregation system in the North and the institutional apartheid system in the South, African American athletes participated in team sports only sporadically and under limited circumstances. Physical educators, coaches, and trainers advanced a number of theories in explaining the segregation of nonwhite players in sports and institutions that in principle were secular, universal, open, and public.

Since the genesis of the industrial era in American history, scientific racism consistently shaped and justified the subordination and exclusion of groups into various spaces of public life. Institutions of higher education were definitely not exempted from or immune to such ideological biases. Quite the contrary, in some instances higher education officials and authorities embraced these principles and presented them in sophisticated formats, which mirrored the outcomes of scientific research. The trajectory and contributions of Elmer D. Mitchell in the 1910s and 1920s illustrate this pattern. Originally, a baseball player and baseball coach for the University of Michigan in the 1910s, Mitchell actively participated in the consolidation of physical education in public universities and the introduction of intramural athletics as institutional policy for all students, pioneered by Michigan and Ohio State in 1913.

As a physical education faculty member and intramurals director, Mitchell published a pioneering work on the benefits of intramural athletics in school in 1925[174] and coauthored another book, *The Theory of Organized Play: Its Nature and Significance,* with Wilbur P. Bowen. Both books enjoyed wide popularity among physical educators and were printed in several editions.[175]

Mitchell published an essay in the *American Physical Education Review* on the connections between race and athletics entitled "Racial Traits in Athletics." His introduction established relationships between organized play, school sports and the general principles of American education:

> Team games and democracy are inseparable, the one goes with the other as a training for free citizenship. ... The playground and the community social center are the greatest factors in Americanization to-day. ... Nowhere, does it seem to me, can we find people closer and truer to their fundamental character than in their free and spontaneous play.[176]

For Mitchell, athletics presented a platform in which different races could successfully advance toward full assimilation, thorough Americanization, and effective adaptation to American industrial life and democratic institutions. Team work, self-sacrifice, cooperation, discipline, and loyalty were all values displayed in the field that inculcated the attitudes that democratic citizenship requires.

> Team games and democracy are inseparable, the one goes with the other as a training for free citizenship. ... It is the Hungarian, the Pole, the Russian Jew, who are disturbing factors in the maintenance of discipline. These nationalities have never had any practice in self-discipline, not even any experience in team play, and when allowed free rein, they gang together in destructive moods. To make orderly citizens of this material is a hope that the playground is striving to realize. The playground and the community social center are the greatest factors in Americanization to-day.[177]

School athletics also constituted a mirror to reflect the authentic values carried by all nationalities by virtue of their "heredity, environment and disposition."[178] Therefore, athletics were not only a privileged lens to identify the hierarchical structures among races and their organic ranking but also a prophetic indicator of each people's ability to succeed in the Americanization process. The dual nature of athletics, as a promise to fully deliver citizenship values and the work ethic of the industrial world, and a standardized field to measure different nationalities in their potential to become American, clearly reveals the privileged position of organized sports in the Progressive Era's national landscape.

As a physical education professor, groomed in the moral and civic benefits that the playground movement identified in sports, Mitchell considered professional and intercollegiate competitions a crucial space to observe, identify, categorize, and appraise a racial classification, a hierarchical structure in which each group would have its place. As a progressive reformer and leading authority in organized sports for regular students, the assessment and categorization of each race and nationality's potential for American citizenship and democratic values was an educational duty and a national priority. Good athletes make good citizens, but Mitchell argued that not every race had the same natural abilities, character and cultural traditions to excel in the contemporary world. From this perspective heredity, environment (physical and social) and determination became new categories for racial stratification in the playground, the school gym, and intercollegiate sports.

The author's methodology relied heavily on his "own experience as a player and as a coach, and from discussions with other men who have had a long experience in athletic coaching."[179] In addition the essay used printed sources on "human races", especially the writings by Albert Gehring (1908),[180] Booker T. Washington (1915),[181] and Daniel G. Brinton (1890).[182]

From a perspective consistent with the Progressive Era, frequent juxtaposition of race, nationality, stock, and people as categories of social analysis and government classification,[183] Mitchell elaborated a detailed hierarchy of human groups according to their contributions to American athletics, both in professional and intercollegiate spheres. His categorization follows a rational instrumentation of principles by which some groups had essential advantages over others while the less able groups had limited or no potential to advance, due to an inability to assimilate in the world of American athletics and American society. For instance the American race was

> a composite of many races; conspicuously the English, Irish, German and Scandinavian. The other races, although now [1922] numerous in our country, have been too recent immigrants as yet to affect our American personality; also because the Southern European races are less readily assimilable.[184]

The American athlete was at the top in the Mitchell athlete-citizen hierarchy. According to *Racial Traits,* heredity, environment, and determination were all in favor of American supremacy in Olympic meets and international competitions:

> The American training methods are the most progressively modern and scientific. The American is willing to train when team winning is

at stake. The American has the physical vigor of a hustling environment, and the confidence which comes from masterful success. ... Not only has he the superior methods, but he has superior material. The sturdy, self-reliant, and tenacious disposition, which he has inherited from his English-speaking forefathers has been "pepped up," made more noisy and cheery, more easy of comradeship, by the addition of an Irish strain; and added to this is Teutonic patience under discipline, and in the mastering of details, which, without the assimilation of German and Swede, would be missing.[185]

Mitchell's characterization of African American students and athletes was certainly shaped by this amalgamation of traditional and "progressive" prejudices:

The negro, as a fellow player with white men, is quiet and unassertive; even though he may be the star of the team he does not assume openly to lead. I have seen cases though where such a star player, if allowed authority, quickly assumed an air of bravado.

The last trait, however, is missing when the negro plays on a team composed of members of his own race, as is often the case in baseball, where the professional leagues have barred him from their ranks. Then he is an inferior athlete, because many things crop out to handicap his natural skill. One of this is the tendency to be theatrical or to play to the grandstand, a trait that the presence of white men suppresses. ...

Many coaches say that the negro is "yellow," that he is good only to a certain point and fails in a crisis. They further add that the negro shows instability and for this reason cannot be relied upon for the big games. Personally, while I think that there is truth in the charge of instability, I do not think that the negro lacks the fighting or the bravery of the white. The reason for what seems to be an apparent failure to play up to his normal standard in the heat of a big game seems to me not that the negro is failing to give his best, but that the white is playing above par. This peculiarity of the white to excel and outdo himself, in critical strife, and to force himself when tired, is explained by the surplus of nervous energy with which nature has endowed him. The negro, lacking this nervous make-up which often makes a weakling white seem strong, seems to be lagging behind men whose efforts normally he could equal, or surpass.[186]

Mitchell's racialized hierarchy of athletic potential and preconditions to assimilate into white American standards included strong opinions against the viability of certain groups:

The racial vitality of the Jew is a wonderful thing when we take into consideration that he has not the physical strength of other races, and that persecutions have followed him through the ages. This vitality is partly explained by the sacredness of family ties among the Hebrew race, and by their clannishness; but more particularly by their adaptability to the bustle and change of modern commercial life. The Jew thrives amidst the tense environment of competitive business and city strain. ... The average Jew is an unpopular team-mate. He is self-assertive, individualistic and quarrelsome. This quarrelsome trait can be easily seen by watching a group of Hebrew children on the playground. Their vigorous assertions of self-opinion, tending to break up team unity, and unqualified leadership become amusing, especially so when they incline to criticize others for their own mistakes.[187]

Race and Athletics: William Montague Cobb and Jesse Owens

William Montague Cobb presented a strong rebuttal of scientific and journalistic accounts that linked victories in sports with geographic, racial, or national "characteristics" in the spirit of Elmer Mitchell and others. Cobb rejected the notion that explained sports differences according to national character, racial features, or ethnic factors and lamented that contemporary media and scientists did not hesitate to assert such links without empirical evidence. Examples of such behavior abounded in boxing, tennis, distance running, and other sports.[188]

As African American athletes emerged as considerable competition in the 1910s and 1920s in track and field, the racialization of their victories associated their new athletic predominance to physical features of the "Negro race," especially limbs, feet, heels, and others. Cobb's analysis tested these connections with specific empirical data from African American elite runners and jumpers, and gathered significant information on black college and Olympic athletes between 1910 and 1932. His findings completely rejected the association between racial features and athletic supremacy:

> We have seen that the variability of the physical, physiological, and personality traits of great sprinters and jumpers, and inadequate scientific data prevent a satisfactory statement as to just what traits are responsible for their success. We have seen also, the importance of training and incentive. Let us now go to the anthropologist. He has to deal with men categorically designated as American Negroes, but they do not look alike. Genetically we know they are not constituted alike. There is not one single physical feature, including skin color, which all of our Negro champions have in common which would identify them as Negroes.[189]

Moreover, Cobb's research included a detailed analysis of Jesse Owens's physical features:

> No particular racial or national group has ever exercised a monopoly or supremacy in a particular kind of event. The popularity of different events with different groups of people has, and probably always will vary, though not necessarily in the same direction.
>
> Negroes have been co-holders but until Owens not single holders of the world's records for the standard sprints. The split-second differences in the performances of the great Negro and white sprinters of past and present are insignificant from an anthropological standpoint. So are the differences in the achievements of the two races in the broad jump.
>
> The physiques of champion Negro and white sprinters in general and of Jesse Owens in particular reveal nothing to indicate that Negroid physical characters are anatomically concerned with the present dominance of Negro athletes in national competition in the short dashes and the broad jump.
>
> There is not a single physical characteristic which all the Negro stars in question have in common which would definitely identify them as Negroes. Jesse Owens who has run faster and leaped farther than a human being has ever done before does not have what is considered the Negroid type of calf, foot, and heel bone.[190]

Figure 6.1 Jesse Owens, Olympic Games 1936 in Berlin.

Cobb's research findings represent a significant step in the implosion of race-based ideologies as central elements in sports performance and physical education. The association between physical performance and racial "traits" receded as a prominent explanatory theory persisted for decades in media portrayals of African American athletes and other nonwhite players.

In organized sports, however, the racialization of athletes of color as "non-team" players, "undisciplined," or "prone to choke" continued to shape and inform decisions by coaches and officials. Even as late as the 1960s, traditional coaches would show resistance to include athletes of color, though they would rarely speak about this in public arenas.

The Color Line and the Gentleman's Agreement

In the 1920s, intersectional games (matches between teams from different conferences) became a regular feature for programs in contention for the national title. As Southern teams increased their participation in football and took proactive steps to build competitive teams, their inclusion in intersectional competitions represented a challenge for the status quo. If a Southern team hosted an intersectional contest, nonwhite athletes on the visiting team would be automatically banned from the game. On the other hand, if a Southern team was the visiting squad, the standard would be that the hosting team would "honor" the tradition of the visitors and exclude its black players from the contest. As a result of this gentleman's agreement, games between Northern and Southern teams regularly excluded black players regardless of the site of the event. A common misconception identifies this agreement as being in effect only when Southern teams hosted games against Northern teams. In reality, the gentleman's agreement applied in most of the games where one of the teams had an all-white ethnic composition.[191]

Big Ten Conference teams featured black players in their football squads with more regularity between 1920 and 1945, some even in prominent positions: William Bell at Ohio State, Willis Ward at the University of Michigan, Jesse Babb and Fitzhugh Lyons at Indiana University. Michigan State included William Baker and Tim McCrary, although Charles Bachman, the coach between 1935 and 1945, benched nonwhites in the games against Mississippi State and Kentucky.

In 1940, NYU students protested against the coach's decision to bench star fullback Leonard Bates in the game with the University of Mississippi. The "Bates Must Play" campaign exposed the school allegiance to the "gentleman's agreement," generating a considerable debate on campus and in New York City. Bates did not participate in the game. The school authorities decided to stay the course and retaliated in 1941 by suspending seven of the students who protested.[192]

In 1947, Michigan State University (MSU) coach Clarence Munn benched Horace Smith for the game against Mississippi State, following the gentlemen's agreement standard protocol. The NCAAP Detroit chapter protested this additional example of "integrated segregation" and petitioned the governor's office to investigate racial discrimination in the Spartan football program. MSU president John Hannah announced that MSU would no longer honor the agreement.

In the 1950s, as the civil rights movement progressed in the South and elsewhere, public universities in the Great Lakes area led the country in recruiting athletes, white or black, based on their merit and potential. In 1955 Illinois, Indiana, and Michigan State had the highest number of black players on their rosters, while Ohio State, Michigan, Wisconsin, Purdue, and Iowa followed not far behind. Clarence Munn established a solid network to recruit African American players from the region and outside, featuring them in key positions. In 1955, Duffy Daugherty, Munn's successor as MSU head coach, recruited Karl Perriman from Alabama, setting a new trend that connected the program with high schools in the South with prominent athletes who could not attend Southern universities.

In the 1950s, public and private universities expanded their recruiting practices to include African American athletes, although still following the principles of exclusion for key positions (quarterback first and foremost) and "stacking," that is, limiting the participation of black football players to a reduced number of starting roles. Despite these practices, Syracuse University produced the first African American Heisman Trophy winner, Jim Brown, who eventually became a superstar as a professional player for the NFL.

The Southeastern Conference followed the national trends on integration reluctantly and several years after. In 1967, Nat Worthington started with the University of Kentucky, although an injury against Old Miss sidelined him early in the season. By the late 1960s, other teams in the conference included African Americans on their rosters, but not in key positions, basically reproducing the "integrated segregation" model prevalent in other conferences before World War II. University of Alabama led the conference in integrating African Americans as key players after being voted third in the National Championship AP Poll in 1966. Notre Dame and Michigan State topped Alabama in votes with the 10-10 historic tie in the "game of the century".[193] Alabama had finished the season both undefeated and untied and many fans and critics took third place as a sign that an all-white team would not be favored, all things being equal, when compared with an integrated squad. The tipping point was the 1970 Alabama-University of Southern

California match in Birmingham. The fully integrated visiting team trounced the all-white Crimson Tide 42–21 on their own turf. Legendary coach Paul "Bear" Bryant initiated a process to integrate the program and recruit talented black athletes from the region that would otherwise migrate to other conferences in the country. John Mitchell was the first African American to play for Alabama in 1971.[194]

Tennessee State and Wilma Rudolph

In the 1950s, the competition between the Soviet Union and the United States intensified at every level in the international arena. Institutions of higher education participated in the Cold War race not only by establishing centers and programs to study every region in the world and generate models for economic development and international collaboration, but also elite programs to develop high-performance athletes to counteract the Soviet hegemony in sports.

Tennessee State University, a historically black college institution, developed a program to produce elite women sprinters under the direction of Edward S. Temple, an outstanding coach and sociology professor. Tennessee State organized its first women's track team in 1946, and in 1948 two of the team's runners made the US Olympic team. The Tennessee State Women's Track Club produced its first gold medal in the 1952 Olympic Games in Helsinki with fifteen-year-old Barbara Jones. Temple's teams dominated track events and won thirty-four national titles, thirty medals in the Pan American Games, and twenty-three in the Olympic Games.[195] Temple coached the US track team in 1958 for the first US-Soviet meet and became a legendary figure with the Tiger Belles athletic successes. Tennessee State female sprinters dominated in the 1950s and 1960s with stars such as Mae Faggs Star, Isabelle Daniels, Edith McGuire Duvall, Martha Hudson Pennyman, Lucinda Williams Adams, Wyoma Tyus, and Madeline Manning Mims, among others.

Wilma Rudolph was born in Tennessee in 1940 to a family with eight children. Her father was a railroad worker and her mother a maid for white families. She had a difficult childhood, plagued by sickness, including polio, and grew up with partial leg paralysis.

Rudolph attended a summer camp event organized by Tennessee State University, became a member of their track team and in 1956 competed in the national championships in Philadelphia. That same year, she participated in the Olympic trials in Washington, DC, and joined the team for the Olympic Games in Melbourne, Australia. Rudolph won a bronze medal (4x100 relay). Her athletic career flourished in 1959, when she won three national sprint titles and set a world record for the 200 meter. She and her Tiger Belles teammates dominated the Olympic trials in Abilene, Texas, in 1960, while her coach, Ed Temple, became the US Olympics coach for women's track and field.

She was the star of the 1960 Olympic Games in Rome, dominating in all her races and winning three gold medals, including a first for the United States in the women's 4x100 relay. Her performance astonished international media, as she broke the world records in 100-meter, 200-meter, and 4x100 relay. Rudolph became the first American woman to win three gold medals in Olympic history. After the games, the track and field team toured Europe, reaching instantaneous celebrity both in Europe and the United States, which included a visit to the White House to meet President Kennedy in 1961.[196]

Figure 6.2 Wilma Rudolph in the lead, Olympic Games 1960 in Rome.

The Revolt of the Black Athlete

Black athletes overcame enormous obstacles for decades in order to participate in team sports at the top college level. By the 1960s, they had momentum on their side, despite fierce opposition by institutional and informal mechanisms in the South and nationwide.

The Texas Western all-black starting lineup shocked the nation and specialized media by defeating the all-white University of Kentucky basketball team in 1966; the Miners dominated the Kentucky top-ranked team 72–65 in the final match. In 1965 and 1966, Michigan State earned national championships (shared with Alabama and Notre Dame) with a predominantly African American lineup. With the athletic success of African Americans in college sports, many universities decided to integrate their competitive programs and engaged in proactive recruiting strategies, generating a substantial increase in the number of black players but without addressing the legacies of discrimination and segregation that black students had been traditionally subjected to in the past.

In 1960, Harry Edwards was recruited by San Jose State to compete in track and field. A prominent "track school," San Jose State reflected many of the inconsistencies and disparities public schools displayed in the treatment of black athletes and black students in general. Edwards faced discrimination in housing, differential treatment in academics, rejection by fraternities and Greek life, discrimination in recreational facilities, segregation in social activities, and so on. After earning a master's degree at Cornell University, Edwards returned to San Jose State as a faculty member, only to discover that treatment for professors of color was no different than what he had witnessed as a student athlete. Resolved to confront the racial inequalities in higher education, Edwards led a movement to activate social change through various means.

In February 1968, the New York Athletic Club (NYAC) celebrated its one-hundredth anniversary track meet at the recently rebuilt and reinaugurated Madison Square Garden. Edwards called for a boycott of the event, arguing the NYAC exclusive membership had never included African Americans. Targeting a signature track event with national and international stars was certainly a challenge, but the boycott was a remarkable success, with most of the elite competitors pulling out, including teams with white athletes and international competitors.

> As the meet dragged on, Edwards called his supporters together outside for a final speech. "You people who want to go inside," he began, "you can go ahead and get your heads busted. But as for me, I think we should go up to Harlem and be with our brothers. The boycott has succeeded, the New York AC is dead. Why stay around here. There are no black brothers here."[197]

Edwards's bigger goal, however, was to address the racial segregation in American sports in addition to inequalities for people of color in athletics in the broader context of colonialism and racial discrimination around the globe. The Olympic Games in Mexico City provided an ideal stage. Starting in 1967, the Olympic Project for Human Rights had called for a boycott of the 1968 Olympics in solidarity with Ethiopia and Algeria, which had dropped out after the International Olympic Committee (IOC) accepted the participation of South Africa in the games. After mounting international pressure, the IOC and Mexico's organizing committee withdrew the invitation to South Africa and Rhodesia. While the international boycott of the Olympic Games dwindled once the apartheid countries were left out, the Olympic Project for Human Rights

(OPHR) continued to call for the boycott by American athletes. The proposal proved to be a divisive issue for college athletes who had been preparing for years to participate in the games. Numerous athletes took a stand in favor and against the boycott, forcing the OPHR to change positions and desist from the boycott yet made the decision to voice their grievances within the games. It was in this context that after the 200-meter finals, gold medalist Tommie Smith and bronze medalist John Carlos raised their fists in black gloves on the medal podium, displaying the Black Power salute. The picture of Smith and Carlos, taken by John Dominis for *Time* magazine, became the image of the games and the poster for sports activism around the world. Smith and Carlos came from the San Jose State track team and had been involved in athletic activism with Harry Edwards.

The following day the winners in the 400 meters (Lee Evans, Larry James, and Ron Freeman) wore black berets on the podium in a similar display. Other US medal winners joined in their own fashion: Ralph Boston received his award barefoot, while Bob Beamon wore black socks in solidarity. Less known is the fact that both Smith and Carlos were severely punished by US Olympic authorities. Right after the award ceremony, the IOC demanded the suspension of Smith and Carlos and threatened to ban displays of activism by any other American athlete in the games. The US Olympic committee suspended Smith and Carlos, removed them from the Olympic Village, and gave them forty-eight hours to leave Mexico City. They were banned from any Olympic competition.[198]

Figure 6.3 John Carlos, Tommie Smith and Peter Norman on the medal podium, Olympic Games 1968 in Mexico City.

In the 1960s, black athlete activism emerged echoing demands similar to the broad petitions in the civil rights movement and shaping claims in regard to the particular and precarious situation of black athletes and black students in predominantly white universities. Hiring of black coaches, inclusion of black cheerleaders, respect for personal appearance choices, respect for black culture, and inclusion of African American staff workers in the athletic departments and sports facilities were some of the most common demands by athletes in their organized struggle.

Demands by black players in college expressed a wide spectrum of social issues affecting African Americans as athletes and as students. Fourteen black football players at the University of Wyoming decided to wear black bands to protest the Latter-Days Saints' official position to exclude African Americans from becoming ordained ministers. The administration decided to preempt the protest display and prohibited it in strong terms. When the players reacted by refusing to play, they were expelled from the team. The Wyoming "Black 14" created a substantial controversy in the Western Conference, and the players took their struggle to court. Later the courts would support the university's coach and officials and refuse to reinstate the players.[199]

African American athletes engaged in social activism across the country to address racial disparities in athletics and education. In association with black student organizations, black faculty, and civic leaders, athletes participated in several instances of political activity looking for ways to improve the environment in education for African Americans in general. Athletes at Iowa State and Michigan State, just to mention two examples out of many, demanded black cheerleaders, the hiring of African American staff and coaches in the athletic department, the hiring of African American faculty, and the inclusion of classes on African American history and culture.[200]

STUDY QUESTIONS

1. Discuss the limited integration of black athletes in college sports between 1890 and 1920.

2. Define the formal and informal rules for intersectional college games in the 1920s regarding race.

3. Discuss Elmer Mitchell's "scientific" racial characterization of black athletes.

4. Discuss the connections between sports, race, and assimilation according to Elmer Mitchell.

5. Discuss the contributions of William Montague Cobb to the study of race and athletics.

6. Discuss the main changes in racial integration in the 1950s.

7. Discuss Harry Edwards's experiences as an athlete and professor at San Jose State University.

8. Discuss the experiences of black athletes in college on and off the field.

9. What were the goals of the Olympic Project for Human Rights (OPHR)?

10. Discuss the boycott of the New York Athletic Club by the OPHR.

11. Discuss the boycott of the Mexico City Olympics by the OPHR.

12. Discuss current examples of social activism by black athletes.

ADDITIONAL READINGS

Cobb, W. Montague. "The Physical Constitution of the American Negro." *Journal of Negro Education* 1, no. 2 (1934): 340–88.

Cobb, W. Montague. "Race and Runners." *Journal of Health and Physical Education* 7, no. 1 (January 1936). http://dh.howard.edu/cgi/viewcontent.cgi?article=1012&context=soci_fac.

Demas, Lane. "Sports History, Race and the College Gridiron: A Southern California Turning Point." *Southern California Quarterly* 89, no. 2 (Summer 2007): 169–93.

Demas, Lane. *Integrating the Gridiron: Black Civil Rights and American College Football.* New Brunswick, NJ: Rutgers University Press, 2010.

Edwards, Harry. *The Revolt of the Black Athlete.* New York: Free Press, 1970.

Hurd, Michael. *Black College Football, 1892–1992: One Hundred Years of History, Education and Pride.* Marceline, MO: Walsworth, 2000.

Martin, Charles H. "Racial Change and 'Big-Time' College Football in Georgia: The Age of Segregation, 1892–1957." *Georgia Historical Quarterly* 80, no. 3 (Fall 1996): 532–62.

Martin, Charles H. "The Color Line in Midwestern College Sports Football in Georgia: The Age of Segregation, 1892–1957." *Indiana Magazine of History* 98, no. 2 (June 2002): 85–112.

Miller, Patrick B. "The Anatomy of Scientific Racism: Racialist Responses to Black Athletic Achievements." *Journal of Sport History* 25, no. 1 (Spring 1998): 119–58.

Mitchell, Elmer D. "Racial Traits in Athletics." *American Physical Education Review* 27, no. 4 (April 1922): 20–21.

Smith, J.M. "Breaking the Plane: Integration and Black Protest in Michigan State University during the 1960s." *Michigan Historical Review* 33, no. 2 (Fall 2007): 101–29.

FIGURE CREDITS

Figure 6.1: Source: https://commons.wikimedia.org/wiki/File%3AJesse_Owens3.jpg.

Figure 6.2: Source: https://commons.wikimedia.org/wiki/File:Giuseppina_leone.jpg.

Figure 6.3: Source: https://commons.wikimedia.org/wiki/File%3AJohn_Carlos%2C_Tommie_Smith%2C_Peter_Norman_1968cr.jpg.

7

College Sports and Mass Media, 1900–1990

Introduction

This chapter analyzes the history of college sports and media from the early telegraph and telephone broadcasting days to the satellite/fiber-optic multimedia era. It traces the rules and foundations of broadcasting sports on network radio and television, the creation of new forms of "packaging" college sports, and the increasing influence of media in college and professional sports. It analyzes the impact of commercial radio, network television, and cable/satellite technologies on the dissemination of college sports content and the popularization of college sports as a unique spectacle for mass consumption.

Moreover, this chapter focuses on the changes and transformations of the ways media corporations, the NCAA, individual programs, and conferences have established and modified economic partnerships according to their own interests and perspectives.

Telegraph, Telephone, and Grid Graphs

Contrary to common assumptions, wire broadcasting of college sports preceded the arrival of commercial radio broadcasting in the 1920s. Since the first decade of the twentieth century, student organizations devised innovative strategies to transmit football games in as much detail as the existing technology would allow. Following the trend set by newspapers and wire news, student football fans used telegraph and telephone lines to transmit live information of games on a play-by-play basis. These quasi-live broadcasts were orchestrated in coordination with telephone and telegraph companies.

The University of Michigan football fans followed the away games in the 1890s by watching a scoreboard created by the *Michigan Daily*, a student newspaper that posted results as soon as they were received by wire communication.[201] On October 31, 1903, a quasi-live broadcast system came into existence in Ann Arbor to cover the Michigan-Minnesota game in Minneapolis. With the collaboration of the Western Union and Bell companies, Floy "Jack" Mattice, a Michigan student and telegraph worker, broadcast the game from a wooden tower built at midfield. The voice signal was received at University Hall Auditorium, where students could have access to the broadcast for a twenty-five-cent fee. The voice transmission was fed to ten telephone lines, allowing students to transcribe the action and then reannounce the information they received through megaphones.[202] The ball position and possession were also charted on a large diagram so everybody could see each drive in almost real time. This innovative system created a permanent link between college sports and fans who could not follow their team in away games.

Figure 7.1 Grid Graph at Hill Auditorium, Michigan vs. Wisconsin, 1923.

In the 1910s, Michigan football broadcasting needed a larger venue and moved to Hill Auditorium, with a more elaborate gridiron board. By the 1920s, the "grid graph" became even more sophisticated, with players' names lighting up according to their participation in a given play. Games were also broadcast to local venues in Ann Arbor and Detroit. The grid graph premiered on October 11, 1924, at the Michigan-Michigan Agriculture College game, which was broadcast on both telephone and radio. The game marked the inauguration of the first steel-and-concrete stadium in East Lansing College Field.[203]

Radio Broadcasting for Student Populations

In the 1910s, universities and private corporations developed broadcasting technologies, which explored the medium potential at various levels, including intercollegiate sports. In 1912, 9X1WLB of the University of Minnesota broadcast a local football game, while the Radio Broadcasting Act established the legal framework for licenses, time limits, and wavelength distribution for commercial radio stations. In 1916, Westinghouse engineer Frank Conrad obtained a license for 8XK, which began broadcasting from Pittsburgh in 1919.[204]

The parallel development of radio broadcasting technologies between universities and private companies set the stage for the emergence of college football broadcasting by college stations and local commercial radio across the country. In the 1920s, dozens of universities successfully filed for radio station licenses and incorporated football games in their programming. Research by Ronald A. Smith has established that Texas A&M station WTAM is incorrectly credited with the first football broadcast in 1920, while the Pitt-West Virginia broadcast in 1921 is recognized as the first college game with a commercial sponsor.[205]

Commercial radio stations also incorporated college football in their programming and played a major role in the popularization of college teams in metropolitan areas. In the 1920s, WGN in Chicago, for instance, broadcast Big Ten games of Penn, Nebraska, and Southern California, while Ivy League matches featuring Harvard, Yale, Princeton, and others were regularly covered in New York City and the urban Northeast.[206] The regional rivalry between Ivy League teams and Big Ten or Western programs provided a unique opportunity for radio stations from New York to Chicago to feature games for mass consumption through the airwaves. In 1922, Princeton's visit to Chicago reached the New York City market via phone lines, and in 1925 the Rose Bowl featuring Southern California and Notre Dame became a hit in the same market.[207] The NBC network broadcast on January 1, 1927, was the first coast-to-coast coverage for the Alabama-Stanford match.[208]

Commercial radio made substantial progress in the 1920s to offer college football as one of the primary choices in sports entertainment. While MLB games and boxing matches also received significant coverage, college football had no rival in the fall as an entertainment choice for an increasing number of American households.

The Great Depression (1929–1933) considerably affected radio broadcasting of college football. Declining attendance rates at the stadiums forced institutions to reconsider the relationship between college athletics and commercial broadcasting. Conferences and programs struggled to find consistent ways to neutralize the impact of the economic recession on attendance and made efforts to shift away from broadcasting the game on radio at the expense of the revenue at the gate. This protectionist perspective proved to be more popular as the financial crisis spread from the stock market and banks into manufacturing and entertainment.

Following protectionist principles, the Eastern Conference banned radio broadcasting of football games in 1930. As early as 1932, the Southern and Southwest Conferences joined the effort with similar bans.[209]

Conference bans on radio broadcasting generated a rift in the NCAA, as some programs realized loss of radio revenue would not automatically translate as an increase in revenue at the football stadium. The NCAA declared that radio broadcasting was "hurting football" in 1932, but established that "home rule" principles should be the standard for broadcasting rules; that is, each institution should decide and negotiate on its own broadcasting contracts regardless of conference regulations. Despite the official "home rule" position, the Southern Conference responded by reasserting the ban for all regular season broadcasts. In 1934, the University of Michigan successfully negotiated radio broadcasting rights with WWJ-Detroit for $20,000, with sponsorship by Chevrolet for all the transmissions. The following year the Big Ten Conference designed a plan to negotiate broadcasting rights for the entire conference. In 1935, the Southern and Southwest Conferences lifted the ban and allowed radio broadcasting to recommence.[210]

Extra-conference games, besides the Rose Bowl, were also able to negotiate their own broadcasting rights. CBS broadcast the 1936 Orange Bowl version for $500.

In 1936, the NCAA reaffirmed the home rule principles and declared radio broadcasting rights the property of universities, not conferences. At the Big Ten the University of Illinois had become the last institution opposing the single package plan. In 1938, school officials lifted the veto on the plan.

By the end of the decade, the radio industry had solidified its partnerships with institutions and conferences to make football a prominent feature on Saturday programming. The participation of school radio stations that covered football in the context of an educational and public service platform entered an irreversible decline. Programs that relied on public university-owned radio broadcasting, like Ohio State or the University of Wisconsin, finally succumbed to big radio corporations, making the broadcasting of football an entirely private and lucrative form of entertainment.[211]

Radio and College Football: An Explosive Cocktail

Radio broadcasting had a substantial growing effect on the number of people connected to college football. As big corporations ventured into commercial radio, mainly NBC and CBS, sports broadcasting reached millions of American households, where entire families were exposed to football rivalries and exaggerated accounts on the relevance and significance of each game. Sporting events became ideal venues to reach millions and capitalize on regional, historical and cultural differences. Radio broadcasting turned college football, a rather elite competition, into a spectacle for mass consumption. Unlike newspaper readership, directed mostly at the head of the household in each family, radio programming was tailored to entire families, gathered in the living room to listen to music, variety shows, and sports.

Figure 7.2 Thundering Herd Meets Irish, advertisement for KHJ radio broadcast of USC-Notre Dame match, 1926.

While live broadcasts originally had to rely on information transmitted from the stadium via telegraph or telephone to the radio station where the broadcasters would reenact the action, the increasing popularity of sports on radio soon made it imperative to broadcast games from a booth on the field.

Soon radio stations began covering college athletics with two broadcasters, a play-by-play announcer and a "color" commentator in charge of providing additional entertainment with stories, anecdotes, jokes, and colloquial phrases. The addition of live broadcast carried by professional storytellers created an unusual bond between listeners and announcers and a deeper connection between fans and the game.

Local radio stations across the country embraced college football as a way to portray the participation of local teams in a national landscape. While MLB franchises before 1945 never featured a city or state west or south of St. Louis, Missouri, college football teams represented every state in the country. For local radio stations the popularization of college football represented a unique opportunity to identify teams with states, cities, and regions in a positive fashion, while emphasizing football as a crucial component of American exceptionalism. Shaping college athletics as representations of American youth, American spirit, national identity, and regional pride therefore became central to the dissemination of sports in radio programming.

Telecasting College Sports

Intercollegiate athletics were the first sports to be covered by network television in American history. On May 17, 1939, the National Broadcasting Company, or NBC, a subsidiary of RCA, broadcast a baseball game between the Columbia Lions and Princeton Tigers at Baker Field in New York City. A doubleheader between the Ivy League rivals is on record as the first sports telecast, even though only the second match was televised and only four hundred television sets in New York were on the receiving end of the signal.[212] The game was narrated by radio personality Bill Stern, and the action was followed by a camera on the stands of the third base line. The viewer's experience must have been quite different from today's standards, due to the black-and-white signal, the camera's inability to follow the ball in continuous shots, and the lack of adequate resolution.[213] The New York Times provided modest reviews of the telecast, expressing optimism but raising concern about the rather poor quality of the transmission, especially in terms of following the action, since the players looked "like white flies running across the 9-by-12 inch screen."[214]

The Columbia-Princeton game decided on extra innings in favor of the local team, an act that motivated NBC to venture into covering MLB games later that summer and telecast the Brooklyn-Cincinnati game from Ebbets Field. NBC president David Sarnoff explored different sports broadcasting opportunities as the company looked to capitalize on the momentum reached in the New York City World's Fair and its emphasis on the technology of the future.[215] On September 30, 1939, New York City was also the place for the first telecast of a football match, when Waynesburg visited Fordham. The telecast was hosted by NBC, and Bill Stern did the play-by-play narration, while the number of television spectators was estimated to be between five hundred and a rather optimistic five thousand.[216] NBC had two cameras on the field, and the signal was on W2XBS, a station set for the New York City 1939 World's Fair.[217] In 1940, Philco broadcast the Maryland-Pennsylvania game, but World War II placed the connections between television and sports on hold.

The first boom of sports broadcasting on network television did not rely on college football or other intercollegiate competitions. In the 1940s CBS and DuMont also ventured into sports broadcasting, particularly after the success of the inauguration of NBC's Gillette Cavalcade of Sports in 1944. Professional baseball and prizefighting became regular features on network television, with the yearly broadcasting of the World Series from 1947 onward as well as several championships from Madison Square Garden and other indoor arenas.[218]

Notwithstanding, television stations broadcast college football matches with strong fan interest in different areas. In 1947, WBKB in Chicago telecasted local Notre Dame games, while other stations acted accordingly with coverage of Army-Navy and other football classics.[219] The Fighting Irish program successfully negotiated exclusive telecasting rights in 1949 with the DuMont network, while the University of Pennsylvania signed a similar contract with ABC in 1950.[220]

In the 1950s, the massive process of suburbanization by which American households located outside of central cities became a central segment of the middle class generated a substantial demand for entertainment no longer tied to locations in downtown areas. As the amusement industries experienced a decrease in attendance, network television expanded into every single new household. Television sets sold by the millions, and television programming considerably expanded in all directions. Entertainment shows and events for mass consumption, from cinema to circus and opera to baseball, suffered the double impact of suburbanization and network television in the country.

The NCAA and Telecasting Rights

The NCAA played a decisive role in the negotiation of telecasting rights for college athletics from 1950 to 1984 and successfully implemented a quasi-monopoly structure to protect the potential negative impact of network television on gate receipts for all its members. Since Notre Dame and Penn had exclusive and individual contracts with television networks and other major programs like Michigan and Illinois had developed closed-circuit broadcasts to bars and movie theaters, the NCAA had to face the challenge of protecting the attendance rates at the stadium while making sure a profitable partnership with television could benefit most programs.[221]

The NCAA effectively lobbied to negotiate telecasting rights for all members of the organization, following a revenue-sharing format and, more importantly, establishing a limitation to one game a week to protect the attendance in all college football games.[222] In the mid-1950s, the NCAA developed a media campaign to present football as an example of national pride, character building, healthy youth formation, and American exceptionalism. In close connection with the values and principles prevalent in the Cold War, the NCAA efficaciously shaped an image of college athletics as an intrinsic component of American masculinity and American patrimony. According to this line of thought, college football and college sports would not only be promoted but also protected as a national priority.[223]

Acting as a cartel, the NCAA responded to Penn's $250,000 exclusive contract with ABC in 1951 by declaring that no NCAA school would participate in a game with Penn, forcing the program to work with the NCAA TV Steering Committee.[224] Assuming the role of protector of a national patrimony and a sport that significantly contributed to the goals of national security in terms of physical strength, the NCAA regulations faced futile resistance from individual programs in the 1950s. In 1961, the House of Representatives blocked live and taped broadcasts of professional games on Fridays and Saturdays, arguing that college football should be protected, embracing the public image of college football and college sports as American patrimony.[225]

Bring the Viewer to the Event, Not the Event to the Viewer

When ABC successfully secured the broadcasting rights for NCAA football games in 1960, company officials decided to give Roone Arledge creative license to innovate and come up with telecast features that would be more appealing to broader audiences. Arledge, a television show producer with former experience at DuMont and NBC, made a decision to organize the game coverage according to the standards of show business, shifting away from the traditional format of covering an event in a neutral or generic fashion. The Arledge credo for sports telecast was first laid out in a memorandum written to his crew in 1960. The opening paragraph described a set of principles that would create an entirely new way to broadcast college football and, later, every other sport on network television:

> Heretofore, television has done a remarkable job of bringing the game to the viewer—now we are going to take the viewer to the game!
>
> We will utilize every production technique that has been learned in producing variety shows, in covering political conventions, in shooting travel and adventure series to heighten the viewer's feeling of actually sitting in the stands and participating personally in the excitement and color of walking through a college campus to the stadium to watch the big game. All these delightful adornments to the actual contest have been missing from previously televised sports ... all the excitement, wonder, jubilation, and despair that make this America's number one sports spectacle, and a human drama to match bullfights and heavyweight championships in intensity.
>
> In short—WE ARE GOING TO ADD SHOW BUSINESS TO SPORTS![226]

Arledge's ideas about bringing standard principles from show business to the production of a sports telecast, instead of following the traditional network television format inherited from radio, required the incorporation of equipment, techniques, and technologies that focused on the dramatic and human dimensions of the competition while at the same time highlighting the experiences of the spectators as participants in the event. In Arledge's productions, the competition was featured as a human drama with the spectator playing the role of protagonist, which he orchestrated through the use of several cameras covering details from different angles: aerial views projecting the feeling of arriving at the stadium and close-ups on the faces of players, coaches, referees, and fans.

The popularization of college football for American suburban households was an indispensable element for the success of ABC sports productions. Making the game appealing to women and men with no college affiliation became a key element in Arledge's new production strategy:

> We must gain and hold the interest of women who are not fanatic fol-
> lowers of the sport we happen to be televising. Women come to football
> games, not so much to marvel at the adeptness of the quarterback in
> calling an end sweep or a lineman pulling out to lead a play, but to sit
> in a crowd, see what everyone else is wearing, watch the cheerleaders,
> and experience countless things that make up the feeling of the game.
> Incidentally, very few men have ever switched channels when a nicely
> proportioned girl was leaping into the air or leading a band downfield.[227]

The combination of human drama with the coverage of the competition and the multilayered focus on fan reactions and behavior generated a new perspective on watching college football and other sports events that expanded the traditional audiences. Players were introduced in street clothes, to create the feeling of a personal and intimate bond with the viewer, while shots of the stadium's surroundings would attempt to build up excitement as if the viewer were actually attending the game live. The action of the game would be covered from six different angles and then replayed by video recorders at different speeds. Slow-motion replays were used on a regular basis to accentuate the drama of a given play in the field.

Asa Bushnell, head of the NCAA TV committee, gave enthusiastic support to Arledge's new vision, although the sponsors were initially not as receptive.[228] Arledge's principles became the standard for ABC and later for the two other major networks, CBS and NBC.

The increasing appeal of college sports on television in combination with the NCAA's exempt status to negotiate broadcasting rights as a single unit produced a substantial expansion on the revenue generated from commercial television. In 1951, broadcasting rights didn't pass the $1 million mark ($679,800), while in 1961 they increased to above $3.1 million. By 1971, the figure reached $12 million, and in 1981 more than doubled hitting $31 million.[229] The 1960s experienced a vast expansion in sports viewership as the Arledge production school spilled over to other networks. The 1966 "Game of the Century" between MSU and Notre Dame, a season final match between two undefeated teams in top rankings, became a de facto championship match and ended in an unprecedented 10–10 tie. The game surpassed high expectations, becoming a classic and opening the door to college football as mass entertainment for American households nationwide.[230]

Deregulation, March Madness, Cable, and Big Time College Sports, 1984–2016

The US Supreme Court ruled in the 1984 landmark case *NCAA v. Board of Regents* that the NCAA had no authority to negotiate broadcasting rights as a single organization for all its members. NCAA protectionist arguments for gate revenues and revenue sharing were rejected by the court, which allowed for individual programs to be entitled to establish their own telecast contracts according to the rules of the free market.[231] Led by the University of Oklahoma, the University of Georgia, and later the College Football Association formed in 1977 by the sixty-two top schools in the sport, the institutional struggle to terminate NCAA's unique position in regard to college football telecasts provided elite programs with great opportunities to shape their own contracts with the big networks. Conferences also strengthened their ability to set their own standards as separate entities.[232] In a simultaneous development with deregulation on cable television and the exponential expansion of satellite communication, college football experienced an unprecedented economic bonanza, affecting mostly, but not exclusively, the elite programs and powerful conferences nationwide.

No longer having control over football, including regular season and end-of-the-year bowls, the NCAA attempted to reinvigorate the organization by revamping the national basketball tournament. Starting in 1939 as a pale shadow of the National Invitational Tournament (NIT) that featured the best teams in the country by bringing them together to Madison Square Garden in New York City, the NCAA national tournament followed a rather modest format, inviting few teams from different conferences to a direct-elimination format that copied the NIT's structure. Since its origin in 1939, the tournament featured eight teams. In the early 1950s, the competition expanded to sixteen teams. In the 1970s thirty-two teams attended, and in 1985 the sixty-four-team format was implemented. Key developments in the first expansion of the tournament were the criminal investigations in 1950–1951 involving point shaving within the New York area teams, along with the investigation of University of Kentucky players participating in similar schemes.

By the 1970s, the NCAA tournament was indisputably the most attractive college basketball competition, so network television participated in the broadcast of final games. A crucial moment for the general interest in the competition took place in 1979 when the Indiana State Sycamores played the Michigan State Spartans in the final match. The rising interest of the two leaders (Larry Bird and Earvin "Magic" Johnson) generated the highest ratings in history for a college basketball event. As a television producer put it:

> It was a giant leap forward for basketball. It catapulted the game into the 80's.[233]

The concept of March Madness, as applied to basketball, was developed by Henry V. Porter, a teacher, basketball coach, and official for the Illinois High School Athlete magazine in March 1939. The Illinois High School Association received trademark ownership for the term in the 1980s.[234] In the mid-1980s, March Madness would become a signature event for intercollegiate athletics featuring the sixty-four best teams of the country playing direct-elimination matches in various cities to finally converge in a single city to determine the national champion.

In 1984, the city of Seattle hosted the semifinal and final matches of the tournament at the Kingdome, an impressive indoor multipurpose stadium. Bob Walsh, a local television producer, marketing strategist, and sports event organizer, in his capacity as executive director of the Final Four Hosting Committee, developed an energetic marketing campaign for the event and the city, drawing parallels with the Super Bowl and other sports television mega-events. In the middle of a legal dispute that finally would turn against the NCAA regarding football broadcasting rights, the organization refocused in the 1980s to make March Madness its signature event with marketing strategies and economic goals similar to big professional contests, namely the Super Bowl.[235]

Marginalized by telecast contract negotiations of individual programs and conferences in regard to football, the NCAA turned the college basketball final tournament into its most advertised competition and a super event to showcase the organization and generate most of its revenue. Basketball finals strategically filled the void between the end of the professional football season and the beginning of Major League Baseball, making an event with strong potential for sports fans across the country.

STUDY QUESTIONS

1. Discuss the various ways sports information was transmitted to student populations before the arrival of radio commercial broadcasting in the 1920s.

2. Explain the participation of university-owned radio stations in football broadcasting.

3. Discuss the pros and cons of radio broadcasting of college athletics in the 1930s.

4. Describe the overall impact of radio broadcasting on college sports between 1920 and 1940.

5. Explain the NCAA policies regarding football telecasting between 1951 and 1984.

6. Discuss the arrival of television show producers to the telecasting of college sports in the 1960s and its significance.

7. Explain Roone Arledge's innovations to college football broadcasting in the early 1960s.

8. Describe the effects of the Arledge school in sports television broadcasting.

9. Discuss the main effects of telecommunication deregulation on the broadcasting of intercollegiate football and basketball.

10. Describe the connections between March Madness and network television.

11. Discuss the overall impact of network television on college revenue sports between 1984 and the current year.

ADDITIONAL READINGS

Arledge, Roone. *Roone: A Memoir.* New York: HarperCollins, 2003.

Edgerton, Gary R. *The Columbia History of American Television.* New York: Columbia University Press, 2007.

Koppett, Leonard. *Baker Field: Birthplace of Sports Television.* http://www.college.columbia.edu/cct_archive/spr99/34a.html.

The Lost Century of American Football. Reports from the Birth of the Game. A Collection of Rare Articles & Illustrations Originally Published in the 19th Century. The Lost Century of Sports Collections. 2011.

"The Michigan Stadium Story. The First 'Broadcast' of U of M Football." Bentley Historical Library, University of Michigan, April 15, 2007. http://bentley.umich.edu/athdept/stadium/stadtext/mattice.htm.

Montez de Oca, Jeffrey. "A Cartel in the Public Interest: NCAA Broadcast Policy During the Early Cold War." *American Studies* 49, no. 3/4 (Fall/Winter 2008): 157–194.

O'Toole, Kathleen M. "Intercollegiate Football and Educational Radio: Three Case Studies of the Commercialization of Sports Broadcasting in the 1920s and 1930s." PhDdiss. Pennsylvania State University, 2010.

Smith, Ronald A. *Play-by-Play: Radio, Television and Big-Time College Sport*. Baltimore: Johns Hopkins University Press, 2001.

Vander Voort, Eric. "First Televised Football Game Featured Fordham, Waynesburg in 1939." National Collegiate Athletic Association, September 29, 2015. http://www.ncaa.com/news/football/article/2014-09-28/first-televised-football-game-featured-fordham-waynesburg-1939.

FIGURE CREDITS

Figure 7.1: Wystan Stevans, "Grid Graph at Hill Auditorium, Michigan vs. Wisconsin, 1923," Bentley Historical Library, University of Michigan, Ann Arbor. Copyright © 1923.

Figure 7.2: Source: https://jhgraham.com/2015/08/31/usc-vs-notre-dame-1926/.

8

Big Time College Sports
U-Brand Revenue-Sports

Introduction

This chapter focuses on the recent developments in intercollegiate competitions and their ultimate consolidation as spectacles for mass consumption.
Following the changes of government, deregulation policies for media and
telecommunications in 1980s college football and college basketball engaged
in a broad process of transformative trends that allowed them to become
unique brands in the world of entertainment.

By the early twenty-first century, March Madness, college basketball
regular season, college football regular season, college New Year's Bowls,
and the college championship playoff had become successful brands
through multiple platforms in mass media.

This chapter also addresses the increasing trends in demand for a new
comprehensive reform in the ethics, integrity, organization, and accountability
for all individuals involved in university athletics. While voices for change and
reform have been a constant in the history of college sports, recent trends
have questioned the role of revenue sports programs in institutions of higher
education from an updated perspective that reflects recent transformations
in universities and society at large. With the consolidation of intercollegiate
athletics as highly profitable sports brands, the social scrutiny and media
perceptions have become increasingly critical of their mission and organization. Moreover, the still gross gender disparities in college sports, after more
than four decades of Title IX legislation, in combination with several scandals

involving criminal sexual violence and administrative cover-ups are highly problematic features in contemporary higher education athletics.

Spectacle for Mass Consumption and Digital Media

In all of its 100+-year history, college sports has not seen an upheaval as great as the "realignment" that has occurred over the last few years. The Big Ten now (2013) has 14 teams, and the Big 12 has now 10. The Pac 10 is now the Pac 12. The Big East Conference has been reconfigured to include only religiously based institutions, and longtime Midwest independent football power Notre Dame has aligned itself with the Atlantic Coast Conference (ACC). What in the world is going on in college athletics? In a word, television.[236]

Figure 8.1 2015 NCAA bracket for Men's Division I basketball tournament on the JW Marriott Hotel in Indianapolis, Indiana.

In 2016, the NCAA renegotiated its telecast contract for sports broadcasting rights with CBS and Turner at a rate of approximately $1.1 billion per year for a period of sixteen years (until 2032). This sharp increase was a first-ever for sports broadcasting rights as the NCAA March Madness passed the $1 billion mark:

> The NCAA today announced an eight-year extension of its multimedia rights agreement with CBS Sports and Turner, a division of Time Warner, for the Division I Men's Basketball Championship. The new contract extends the agreement through 2032, and ensures that one of the premier American sports events will be telecast by two of the world's preeminent media companies for almost two more decades.[237]

The exclusive deal included broadcasting by CBS and Turner through every digital platform, according to the new standards of digital media. Starting in 2011, the NCAA Basketball Men's Tournament was covered by multiple channels in simultaneous broadcasts. Five years later, live coverage of NCAA men's basketball had doubled, and the number of watching fans substantially increased. In 2016, NCAA president Mark Emmert introduced an unprecedented renegotiation contract as a crucial element in sustaining the institution's mission to sponsor student-athletes nationwide:

> The extension of our current agreement will allow our more than 1,100 NCAA member colleges and universities to continue to support student-athletes on 19,000 teams across 24 sports. We have a diverse membership with varying resource levels, and this extension will assist our campuses as they provide pathways to opportunity in higher education and beyond for nearly a half a million young men and women each year.[238]

Following the most successful marketing and advertising strategies from American and global professional sports organizations, NCAA sponsorships and advertisers are among the top global corporations. NCCAA "elite" partners reflect a well-structured and highly developed brand plan:

> The NCAA is proud to have the elite companies AT&T, Capital One and Coca-Cola as official Corporate Champions, and the following elite companies as official Corporate Partners: Allstate, Amazon Echo, Bing (Microsoft), Buffalo Wild Wings, Buick, Enterprise, Infiniti, LG, Lowe's, Nabisco, Northwestern Mutual, Reese's, Unilever and UPS.[239]

The NCAA contract closely resembles in scope and magnitude broadcasting rights for global professional sports, like the Spanish soccer league La Liga, German professional soccer Bundesliga, the Summer and Winter Olympic Games, and the MLB. According to *Forbes* magazine, which researches the value of sports brands and their evolution on a yearly basis, College Football Playoff and Final Four for Men's Basketball are respectively the sixth and seventh most valuable sports events in the world (with brand value estimates of $160 million for the former and $155 million for the latter).[240]

Ironically, the NCAA is a nonprofit legal entity and a charitable organization with the promotion of amateur college athletics as its main mission.[241] As a charitable organization, the NCAA is entitled to various tax exemptions and a legal status clearly different from any professional sports association.

The ESPN College Football Playoff MegaCast in 2017, featuring Clemson and Alabama under AT&T sponsorship, had fourteen alternative productions to satisfy the unique needs and expectations of large constituencies according to different criteria; in addition to the "traditional telecast" on ESPN, alternative productions simultaneously broadcast the event on ESPN2, ESPNU, ESPN3, ESPNClassic, ESPNDeportes, ESPNRadio, ESPNDeportesRadio, ESPN Goal Line, and the SEC Network.[242] The fourth MegaCast organized by ESPN also provided content through multiple platforms, including social media (Facebook, Instagram, Twitter) and international outlets around the world via ESPN International. The production featured more than ninety cameras inside Raymond James Stadium in South Florida, with more than one thousand staffers on-site.[243]

Figure 8.2 ESPN College GameDays interview with USC Trojans' Matt Barkley in Ohio Stadium, Columbus Ohio, 2009.

More than 26 million people watched the game, consolidating a recent trend in cable television by which College Football Playoff games (starting in 2015) have become the most watched cable telecasts ever.[244] In only three years, the College Football Playoff Championship Game has already become an essential element in the landscape of sports entertainment and sports branding.

College Sports and Public Opinion

> To be sure, big-time college sports mass entertained the American public, but it has all too frequently done so at the expense of our colleges and universities, their students, faculty, and staff, and the communities they were created to serve. They have infected our academic culture with the commercial values of the entertainment industry. They have distorted our priorities through the disproportionate resources and attention given to intercollegiate athletics. They have also distracted and in some cases destabilized the leadership of our academic institutions. They have exploited, and on occasion, even victimized players and coaches while creating a sense of cynicism on the part of the faculty and broader student body. Most significantly, big-time college sports have threatened the integrity and reputation of our universities, exposing us to hypocrisy, corruption, and scandal that all too frequently accompany activities driven primarily by commercial value and public visibility.[245]

In the above statement, which has been quoted broadly, James Duderstadt, former president of the University of Michigan, summarized the central elements of an increasingly critical institutional perspective on revenue sports hosted by institutions of higher education in the 1990s. Since the origins of college sports in the nineteenth century, school officials, reformers, and intellectuals have debated and questioned the presence of organized competition as a form of entertainment inside institutions of higher education. The main critique against college athletics has persistently relied on four principles.

1. Threat to Educational Values

The mere existence of college sports and particularly organized sports for mass consumption interfere with the educational mission of universities. Such characterization constitutes the central core of the 1929 Carnegie Report and has ever since been a foundational stone in the current backlash against college athletics.

2. Commercialism vs. Character Building

Commercialism and capitalist gains have forced intercollegiate athletics to shift away from their original calling to act as a vehicle to shape character, teach discipline and teamwork, and ultimately help youth to become successful adults. The fact that college sports have substantially deviated from their original purposes in subordination to commercial interests represents a potentially irreversible distortion, a concern which has been consistently voiced since the late nineteenth century and has become, in the first decades of the twenty-first century, the central point against intercollegiate competitions, especially football and basketball.

3. The Student-Athlete

The legal status of college players as student-athletes appears dubious, given the contributions that mostly young African American players make to generate revenue for coaches, sports media, the NCAA, universities, global brands, marketing agencies, and sports bureaucracies, without receiving a proportionate dividend from their institutions. The creation of a legal limbo for college players as student-athletes who are remunerated by services, benefits, and expenses, significantly disproportionate to the revenue they generate and the compensation coaches, athletic directors, assistant directors, assistant coaches, and staff ordinarily receive, has in recent years substantially developed into a full argument for the reclassification of student-athletes as workers entitled to form unions and bargain compensation through legal standards.

4. Transparency

The lack of accountability, transparency, and integrity on the part of college sports organizations (NCAA and college conferences) and college sports authorities (university presidents, coaches, athletic directors) has also gained significant momentum in light of media scandals. This argument has been consistently presented with examples of academic fraud, orchestrated systematically by different programs to keep players eligible. Recent developments have strengthened the trend with scandals involving sexual violence and criminal behavior, involving cover-ups by college sports authorities to "protect" the program brand.

Scandals, from Academic to Criminal

Academic and criminal scandals centered on university sports programs have produced a permanent source of outrage and entertainment in contemporary media, as they have received coverage usually assigned to celebrities, professional athletes, and political figures.

While scandals in regard to academic integrity and eligibility standards have been prevalent in recent decades, the most aggravating controversies since the 1990s have been centered on sexual violence and official ineptitude in addressing the problem in a fair, transparent, and systematic manner. Between 1991 and 1995, for example, there were several episodes involving sexual violence perpetrated by University of Nebraska football players.[246]

A gang rape case involving football players and recruits at the University of Colorado in 2001 evolved into additional rape complaints by the only female player in the football program. In 2007 *Simpson v. the University of Colorado,* the school agreed to pay $2.85 million to the plaintiffs, establishing in the courts a precedent for the liability of school administrators and programs for the sexual assaults involving revenue athletes and female students.[247]

Sexual assault cases involving student athletes occur every school year on a regular basis nationwide. The prevalence of sexual violence in connection with athletics, fraternities, and the general student population is becoming a health priority issue for institutions of higher education. School officials have become increasingly aware of the legal, criminal, and financial liabilities they face when addressing such issues in contrast with the more traditional and "old boys network" standards that have served their institutions in the past.[248]

One of the worst episodes in the cycle of college criminal scandals occurred at Penn State University in the first years of the twenty-first century, involving the popular college football coach Joe Paterno, whose record of most wins made him a brand in and of itself. In 2001, a graduate assistant, Mike McQuary, reported to Paterno and school authorities he had seen assistant coach Jerry Sanduski naked with a minor in the school facilities. The reaction of the coach and president, centered on internally handling Sanduski's behavior, left his criminal activities unchecked. Steering the issue away from the attention of the media and authorities only endangered other minors exposed to Sanduski's predatory behavior. When the scandal broke in 2010–2011, Penn State University's Board of Trustees fired Paterno and president Graham Spanier, setting a clear new precedent for coaches, athletic directors, and school presidents nationwide. Penn State University had to pay over $73 million in fines to the NCAA and the Big Ten, plus over $100 million in settlements to the victims.

Ultimately, Sanduski was found guilty on forty-five counts for molesting ten boys and sentenced to thirty to sixty years in prison, while later Penn State ex-president Spanier faced criminal charges of child endangerment and was found guilty.[249]

A New Low: Larry Nassar and Michigan State University

On September 12, 2016, the *Indianapolis Star* reported a breaking news story, involving Rachael Denhollander. The thirty-one-year-old lawyer and former gymnast accused Michigan State University doctor, Lawrence "Larry" Nassar, of sexually abusing her in the year 2000 when she was fifteen years old. Denhollander became the first woman to publicly denounce the criminal behavior of Doctor Nassar.

Besides his appointment as faculty member at Michigan State's College of Osteopathic Medicine, Nassar was a team physician at Twistars Gymnastics Club USA and for the USA Gymnastics Olympic team. In 2015, complaints of sexual abuse against Nassar in USA Gymnastics led to his resignation; nonetheless, Nassar continued to work with girls and women athletes at Michigan State and Twistars.[250]

The *Indianapolis Star* investigative report marked only the beginning of a horrific story of sexual abuse and institutional criminal negligence. Allegations of Nassar's sexual misconduct at Michigan State emerged as early as 1997. Athletes abused by Nassar complained to gymnastics coach Katie Klages and multiple officials, who dismissed the allegations and tried to protect the program's prestige at the expense of the victims. The vast number of complaints led to an official investigation in 2014 that "cleared" Nassar of any wrongdoing. University officials decided to handle the situation internally by recommending that Nassar have a "chaperone" in the room while treating athletes. Despite the institutional inaction, survivors took their claims to criminal and civil courts and bravely defied the corrupt official reactions by Michigan State and USA Gymnastics. Arrested in 2016, Nassar was sentenced to sixty years in prison on federal child pornography charges in 2017.

In January 2018, more than 150 survivors testified in the Ingham County court and told their stories to the world, confronting their victimizer and bringing national and international attention to sexual abuse. Nassar's victims included girls as young as six years old, female gymnasts of various ages, as well as athletes from multiple sports at Michigan State; the most famous were Olympic medalists McKayla Maroney, Jamie Danstzcher, Aly Reisman, Jordyn Wieber, and Simone Biles. The survivor impact statements became much more than legal formalities; the stories received global notice, as they featured young female athletes willing to fight abuse and corruption.

In the words of Kyle Stephens, who was six years old when Nassar began sexually abusing her, "Little girls don't stay little forever. They grow into strong women that return to destroy your world."[251]

On January 24th, 2018, Nassar was sentenced to up to 175 years in prison, in addition to his prior sixty-year sentence in federal court for possession of child pornography. Michigan State University's president Lou Ann Simon was forced to render her unconditional resignation on the very same day. Nassar and Simon's names became instantly linked to the worst criminal scandal in American sports history, while the survivor stories have simultaneously changed the way American media and society look at sexual misconduct and institutional corruption in college sports.

Big-Time College Sports and Reform

In October 2011, Taylor Branch, a prominent public historian, published a wide-ranging critique of intercollegiate sports in the *Atlantic* under the title "The Shame of College Sports." In the article, he presented some of the notorious scandals in a historical context and called for a comprehensive reform.[252] The recent wave in favor of change and modernization in the structure and foundation of college sports has increased in volume and dimension. Notable figures in the milieu have come out with powerful arguments against the status quo and in favor of substantial changes. Walter Byers, the architect of the NCAA as its executive director between 1951 and 1987, published a memoir in 1995 exposing the NCAA's flaws and exploitative relationship with college players.[253] In 2000, James Duderstadt presented a detailed perspective on the main challenges and a possible path to reform.[254]

Likewise, academics have voiced opinions on the subject that fluctuate from a cynical perspective to strong condemnation of intercollegiate athletics in their entirety. In 1999, Andrew Zimbalist, economics professor at Smith College, published *Unpaid Professionals: Commercialism and Conflict in Big-Time College Sports*, providing a comprehensive analysis of college athletics as a sports industry and making a persuasive case on the desperate need for a complete restructuring of the connections between universities and sports.[255]

In 2000, professor Murray Sperber of Indiana University published *Beer and Circus: How Big-Time College Sports Is Crippling Undergraduate Education*. Sperber's analysis of revenue sports echoes the Carnegie Report (1929) findings regarding the overall negative impact that college athletics had on the educational mission of colleges and universities and provides an updated panorama of how corruption and commercialism have come to dominate conferences, programs, and organizations.[256]

Historian Ronald Smith, an authority on the history of sports in American society, published a comprehensive history of reform attempts in college sports from the nineteenth century to the present decades, highlighting the forces acting behind a successful change in the field.[257] As Smith aptly points out in his research, the desire to reform and "clean" college sports is as old as the competitions, and the debate on which direction higher education institutions should follow has been a notable feature for decades, generations, and centuries.

From the 1990s, think-tank programs have brought together scholars, sports journalists, school authorities, and others to produce professional and independent reports on the current status of college athletics and the potential for change. The Knight Commission and the Drake Group represent two notable examples of such efforts. The Knight Commission was founded in 1989:

> The Knight Commission was formed by the John S. and James L. Knight Foundation in October 1989 in response to highly visible scandals in college sports. The Commission's goal is to promote a reform agenda that emphasizes the educational mission of college sports. Over the years, the NCAA has adopted a number of the Commission's recommendations including the rule that requires teams to be on track to graduate more than 50 percent of their players in order to be eligible for postseason competition.[258]

After the Knight Commission, the Drake Group was founded in 1999:

> an organization of faculty and staff who seek to defend academic integrity in college sports. ... The Drake Group was founded in 1999 when a distinguished group of college faculty, authors, and activists were invited to Drake University for a twenty-four-hour think tank in how to end academic corruption in college sport. Included in the conference were members of faculty senates, journalists, athletic directors, and members of organizations such as the NCAA and the Knight Foundation Commission on collegiate Sport.[259]

A romantic idealization of college athletics certainly underscores the nature of such competitions from their origins and throughout history. College sports, mostly but not exclusively football and basketball, have permanently included the most prominent features of professional sports brands, and in many instances, college sports have led the world of professional sports and entertainment with respect to innovative strategies and policies. The first steel-and-concrete stadium in the United States was built in 1903 to house Harvard University football. No other sport, professional or otherwise, could boast a stadium infrastructure similar to the one created for college football in the 1920s. College stadiums were the largest in the country and the largest in the world. To this day, college stadiums are the largest sports venues in the nation.

Similarly, college sports were the first televised in American history (in 1939) and led the country in radio broadcasting in the 1910s and television broadcasting in the late 1940s and early 1950s. The NCAA led the nation as the first sports organization negotiating telecasting rights in a single package in the 1950s. In similar developments, college sports transitioned from network television to cable and digital platforms before their counterparts in any other professional sport. Despite strong claims regarding the excessive influence of media and commercialism in the field, the historical record of college athletics indicates that they have been spectacles for wide and mass consumption from their very beginnings in the nineteenth century, with commercial interests having always been an intrinsic element of the games.

College sports, either following the lead of individual programs, the NCAA, or conferences, have set the trends for innovative partnerships with media corporations to broadcast games. In the latest development of such processes, the Big Ten Conference formalized a 51–49 percent partnership with Fox Entertainment Group in 2006 to create the Big Ten Network (BTN), a cable television corporation with the main purpose of broadcasting Big Ten sports and programming on a regular basis. BTN became the first cable network to showcase college conference games. In doing so, BTN instantly turned the Big Ten Conference into a media corporation and a sports news outlet all by itself. BTN was the first development in this trend, but certainly not the only one. Soon after, Pac-12, ACC, and SEC conferences engaged in the formation of their own cable networks, while other programs pursued the establishment of cable channels to broadcast their home sports individually, such as the Longhorn-Channel (University of Texas) and BYUTVsports (Brigham Young University). Big Ten Network has generated unprecedented revenue for the conference and played a major role in the 2012 expansion plans to include teams from target television markets in New York City and the District of Columbia.[260]

The argument that college sports should go back to their original mission is at best naive and at worst ignorant of the very nature of intercollegiate competitions, which, from their inception, constituted a central element of the mass media and the entertainment industry. The recent developments in the digital era only accentuate the organic and permanent link between college sports and the amusement industries.

The NCAA is the only remaining sports organization that participates in multimedia multimillion-dollar deals while maintaining amateurism as one of its foundational principles. The Amateur Sports Act, signed in 1978 by President Jimmy Carter, opened the door for the professionalization of Olympic athletes in the United States and the ultimate participation of professional competitors in international and Olympic games. Since the 1984 Summer Olympics in Los Angeles, amateur status is no longer part of the Olympic movement.[261] Ironically, NCAA amateur ideals apply to college athletes but not to trainers, coaches, assistant coaches, staff, athletic department personnel, athletic directors, event workers, university presidents, or any of the NCAA authorities and employees.

Figure 8.3 President George W. Bush and University of Texas football coach Mack Brown with the Texas Longhorns football team, Washington D.C., 2005.

Intercollegiate athletics and their multiple and complex links to mass media, technology, human performance research, regional and national identities, and contemporary notions of masculinity have been at the center of debates and controversies over their social role since the beginning of student competitions in the nineteenth century. Waves of reform and transformation have proved the fluid nature of college sports in American society in almost every decade of their existence. As strong symbols of youth, success, power, and fitness, college players have also been consistently subjected to the scrutiny of school authorities, scholars, trainers, reformers, and government officials. Legal battles regarding the nature and status of intercollegiate competitions have also contributed to shaping the social status and profile of players, coaches, and school officials.

The history of intercollegiate athletics has consistently showed their close and complex connections with society and their ability to engage in processes of metamorphosis across time. Since their original days college sports have proved to be a unique mirror to feature the dominant social values and expectations placed on youth, equality, education and the future at large.

STUDY QUESTIONS

1. Discuss the differences and commonalities between the College Football Playoff and other mega-sports events like the Super Bowl or FIFA World Cup.

2. Discuss the differences and commonalities between college revenue sports and professional sports organizations (NBA, NFL, MLB, NHL).

3. Compare the 2017 ESPN Megacast (Alabama-Clemson) with other sports multiplatform productions, like the NBA Finals or the World Series.

4. Explain the current trends against commercialism in college sports.

5. Discuss the partnerships between the Big Ten and media corporations, and the formation of the Big Ten Network.

6. Explain the development of partnerships between media corporations and individual programs like the University of Texas and Notre Dame.

7. Discuss the impact of academic and criminal scandals on college athletics.

8. Explain the main areas where college sports need a vigorous reform according to some scholars, research institutions, and former school officials.

9. How would you modify or reform collegiate athletics in response to the issues identified as most problematic.

10. What, in your opinion, would be the main challenges in reforming intercollegiate athletics?

ADDITIONAL READINGS

Benford, Robert D. "The College Sports Reform Movement: Reframing the 'Edutainment' Industry." *Sociological Quarterly* 48, no.1 (Winter 2007): 1–28.

Holthaus, William D. Jr. "Ed O'Bannon v. NCAA: Do Former NCAA Athletes Have a Case Against the NCAA for Its Use of Likeness?" *Saint Louis University School of Law Journal* (St. Louis, MO) 55 (2010): 369.

Taylor, Branch. "The Shame of College Sports." *Atlantic*, October 2011.

Weaver, Karen. "Media Deals, College Football and Governance: Who Is in Charge?" *Change: The Magazine of Higher Learning* 45, no. 4 (2013): 15–23.

FIGURE CREDITS

ENDNOTES

1. *Wikipedia*, "Jock (Stereotype)," June 17, 2017. https://en.wikipedia.org/wiki/Jock_(stereotype).

2. W. Burlette Carter, "The Age of Innocence: The First 25 Years of the National Collegiate Athletic Association. 1906 to 1931." *Vanderbilt Journal of Entertainment and Technology Law* 8, no. 2 (Spring 2006): 211–291.

3. Kristen R. Muenzen, "Weakening Its Own Defense? The NCAA's Version of Amateurism." *Marquette Law Sports Review* 13, no. 2 (Spring 2003): 257–88, 260. http://scholarship.law.marquette.edu/cgi/viewcontent.cgi?article=1276&context=sportslaw.

4. Howard Savage, with Harold W. Bentley, John T. McGovern, and Dean F. Smiley. *American College Athletics*. Carnegie Foundation for the Advancement of Teaching. Bulletin Number Twenty-Three, New York (1929): 35.

5. *University of Denver v. Nemeth*, 257 P.2d 423 (1953). http://law.justia.com/cases/colorado/supreme-court/1953/16945.html

6. *University of Denver v. Nemeth*.

7. Walter Byers, with Chris Hammer. *Unsportsmanlike Conduct: Exploiting College Athletes*. (Ann Arbor: University of Michigan Press, 2010): 65.

8. *Van Horn v. Industrial Acc. Com.*, Civ. No. 27105. Second Dist., Div. One (1963). http://law.justia.com/cases/california/court-of-appeal/2d/219/457.html

9. *Van Horn v. Industrial Acc. Com.*

10. US National Labor Relations Board, NORTHWESTERN UNIVERSITY Employer and COLLEGE ATHLETE PLAYERS ASSOCIATION (CAPA) Petitioner, Case 13-RC-121359, 2014, 5.

11. NLRB Northwestern University and College Athlete Players Association (CAPA), Petitioner. Case 13-RC-121359. August 17, 2015, 14–18.

12. NLRB Northwestern University and College Athlete Players Association (CAPA), 18.

13. NLRB Northwestern University and College Athlete Players Association (CAPA), 3–4.

14. NLRB Northwestern University and College Athlete Players Association (CAPA), 5.

15. Charles W. Caldwell Jr., *Modern Football for the Spectator*. (Philadelphia: Lippincott, 1953): 23.

16. Ronald A. Smith, *Big Time Football at Harvard, 1905: The Diary of Coach Bill Reid.* (Urbana: University of Illinois Press, 1994): xvii–xviii.

17. Michael Kimmel, *Manhood in America: A Cultural History.* (New York: Free Press, 1996): 117–127.

18. Smith, *Big-Time Football at Harvard, 1905*, xvii.

19. John R. Thelin, *A History of American Higher Education*, 2nd ed. (Baltimore: Johns Hopkins University Press, 2011): 1–40.

20. Howard J. Savage et al., *American College Athletics.* Bulletin No. 73 (New York: Carnegie Foundation for the Advancement of Teaching, 1929): 13–16.

21. Savage, *American College Athletics*, 13–33.

22. Gumprecht, Blake. "The American College Town." *Geographical Review*, 93.1 (2003): 51–80

23. Baird, William R. *American College Fraternities: A Descriptive Analysis of the Society System in the Colleges of the United States.* Philadelphia: J.B. Lippincott & Co., 1879.

24. Guy Lewis, "The Beginning of Organized Collegiate Sport." *American Quarterly* 22, no. 2 Part 1 (1970): 224.

25. Lewis Sheldon Welch and Walter Camp, *Yale: Her Campus, Class-Rooms and Athletics* (Boston: L.C. Page and Company, 1900): 458–512.

26. Ibid.

27. Lewis, "The Beginning of Organized Collegiate Sport," 224.

28. Lewis, "The Beginning of Organized Collegiate Sport," 226–227.

29. Lewis, "The Beginning of Organized Collegiate Sport," 227–228.

30. Lewis, "The Beginning of Organized Collegiate Sport," 228.

31. Ibid.

32. Welch and Camp, *Yale*, 513–515.

33. Welch and Camp, *Yale*, 514–516; Lewis, "The Beginning of Organized Collegiate Sport," 227.

34. Welch and Camp, *Yale*, 451–458.

35. Welch and Camp, *Yale*, 451–453.

36. Clifford Putney, *Muscular Christianity: Manhood and Sports in Protestant America, 1880–1920* (Cambridge, MA: Harvard University Press, 2001): 1–25.

37. Putney, *Muscular Christianity*, 25–44.

38. Putney, *Muscular Christianity*, 174.

39. Putney, *Muscular Christianity*, 21.

40. Putney, *Muscular Christianity*, 64–71.

41. Putney, *Muscular Christianity*, 59–67.

42. Putney, *Muscular Christianity*, 68.

43. Putney, *Muscular Christianity*, 163–165.

44. YWCA, "History," 2017. http://www.ywca.org/site/c.cuIRJ7NTKrLaG/b.7515891/k.C524/History.htm.

45. David Goldblatt, *The Ball Is Round: A Global History of Soccer* (New York: Penguin, 2008): 3–18.

46. Goldblatt, *The Ball Is Round,* 19–50.

47. Ibid.

48. Vernon Scarborough and David R. Wilcox, *The Mesoamerican Ballgame* (Tucson: University of Arizona Press, 1993): 101–125.

49. Parke H. Davis, *Football: The American Intercollegiate Game* (New York: Scribner, 1911): 1–31.

50. Ibid.

51. Davis, *Football,* 30–31

52. Davis, *Football,* 44–50.

53. Ibid.

54. Davis, *Football,* 47–50.

55. Ibid.

56. Ibid.

57. Davis, *Football,* 62–67.

58. Davis, *Football,* 33–43.

59. Davis, *Football,* 34–35.

60. Davis, *Football,* 37.

61. Davis, *Football,* 38.

62. Davis, *Football,* 39.

63. Davis, Football, 39.

64. Davis, *Football,* 37.

65. Davis, Football, 51–74.

66. Ibid.

67. Walter Camp, *American Football* (New York: Harper, 1891): 1–22.

68. Camp, *American Football,* 9–10.

69. Camp, *American Football,* 11.

70. Camp, *American Football,* 19.

71. Camp, *American Football,* 13.

72. Camp, *American Football,* 109–110.

73. Camp, *American Football,* 120.

74. Camp, *American Football,* 126, 135.

75. David L. Westby and Allen Sack, "The Commercialization and Functional Rationalization of College Football: Its Origins." *Journal of Higher Education,* 47, no. 6 (1976): 625–647.

76. John Sayle Watterson, *College Football: History, Spectacle, Controversy* (Baltimore: Johns Hopkins University Press, 2000): 19.

77. Walter Camp, *Danny the Freshman* (New York: Appleton, 1915): 8.

78. Lewis Sheldon Welch and Walter Camp, *Yale: Her Campus, Class-Rooms, and Athletics,* 2nd ed. (Boston: Page, 1900): 26, 338.

79. Camp, *Danny the Freshman*, 7.
80. Harford Willing Hare Powel, *Walter Camp, the Father of American Football: An Authorized Biography* (Boston: Little, Brown, 1926): 160–182.
81. Powel, *Walter Camp, the Father of American Football*, 17.
82. Davis, Parke H. *Football: The American Intercollegiate Game.* New York: Scribner, 1911. 117–118.
83. Ronald A. Smith, "Commercialized Intercollegiate Athletics and the 1903 Harvard Stadium." *New England Quarterly* 78, no. 1 (March 2005): 26–48.
84. John S. Watterson, "Political Football: Theodore Roosevelt, Woodrow Wilson and the Gridiron Reform Movement." *Presidential Studies Quarterly* 5, no. 3 (Summer 1995): 555–564.
85. "Tragedy Marks Union Game. Fatal Injury to Harold Moore: Union '08." *Triangle* 12, no. 7 (November 28, 1905): 1.
86. "Tragedy Marks Union Game," 1.
87. Mark Alden Branch, "A Hundred Years in the Round," *Yale Alumni Magazine*, September/October 2014. https://yalealumnimagazine.com/articles/3942-yale-bowl.
88. Pierson, George W. *A Yale Book of Numbers: Historical Statistics of the College and University* (New Haven: Yale University 1983)
89. Bentley Historical Library, University of Michigan. "University of Michigan Bond." n.d. http://bentley.umich.edu/athdept/stadium/images/umbond.jpg.
90. Fielding H. Yost, *Football for Player and Spectator* (Ann Arbor: University Publishing Company, 1905): 263–272.
91. Yost, *Football for Player and Spectator*, 270–272.
92. John Kryk, *Stagg vs. Yost: The Birth of Cutthroat Football* (Lanham, MD: Rowman and Littlefield, 2015): 48.
93. Ronald A. Smith, *Play-by-Play: Radio, Television and Big-Time College Sport* (Baltimore: Johns Hopkins University Press, 2001): 207–211.
94. Smith, *Play-by-Play*, 18–27.
95. Smith, *Play-by-Play*, 28–34.
96. Smith, *Play-by-Play*, 212–213.
97. Kryk, *Stagg vs. Yost.*
98. Murray Sperber, *Shake Down the Thunder: The Creation of Notre Dame Football* (Bloomington: Indiana University Press, 1993).
99. Kryk, *Stagg vs. Yost.*
100. John W. Heisman, "Inventions in Football." *Baseball Magazine* 1, no. 6 (October 1908): 40–42.
101. Sperber, *Shake Down the Thunder*, 99.
102. Sperber, *Shake Down the Thunder*, 103–115.
103. Sperber, *Shake Down the Thunder*, 118.

104. Sherry C.M. Lindquist, "Memorializing Knute Rockne at the University of Notre Dame: Collegiate Gothic Architecture and Institutional Identity." *Winterthur Portfolio* (University of Chicago) 46, no. 1 (Spring 2012): 1–24.

105. Lindquist, "Memorializing Knute Rockne at the University of Notre Dame," 1–24.

106. Sperber, *Shake Down the Thunder.*

107. For the South Eastern Conference, for example, see Jon. Cooper, "Documenting the Statues on SEC Campuses and Stadiums," *Saturday Down South.* https://www.saturdaydownsouth.com/sec-football/sec-football-statues

108. Adam Kramer, "A Day in the Life of Nick Saban's Statue," *Bleacher Report*, November 11, 2016. http://thelab.bleacherreport.com/a-day-in-the-life-of-nick-sabans-statue

109. "Founded by Andrew Carnegie in 1905 and chartered in 1906 by an act of Congress, the Carnegie Foundation for the Advancement of Teaching has a long and distinguished history. It is an independent policy and research center, whose primary activities of research and writing have resulted in published reports on every level of education." www.carnegiefoundation.org

110. Howard Savage, with Harold W. Bentley, John T. McGovern, and Dean F. Smiley. *American College Athletics* (Carnegie Foundation for the Advancement of Teaching. Bulletin Number Twenty-Three, New York, 1929): 8.

111. Savage, Bentley, McGovern, and Smiley. *American College Athletics,* 4–5.

112. Savage, Bentley, McGovern, and Smiley. *American College Athletics,* 3–33.

113. Savage, Bentley, McGovern, and Smiley. *American College Athletics,* 119.

114. Savage, Bentley, McGovern, and Smiley. *American College Athletics*, 188–89.

115. Savage, Bentley, McGovern, and Smiley. *American College Athletics*, 266–290.

116. Savage, Bentley, McGovern, and Smiley. *American College Athletics*, 308.

117. W.H. Cowley, "Athletics in American Colleges." *Journal of Higher Education* 70, no. 5 (September/October 1999, 1930): 494–503.

118. "Amos Alonzo Stagg Papers." https://www.lib.uchicago.edu/e/scrc/findingaids/view.php?eadid=ICU.SPCL.STAGG

119. NYU University Archives, "Athletics: Football," Group 41.4 Series No.2 Box No. 37 Folder Football Policy/Discontinuation. 1941. Folder 1.

120. Ronald A. Smith, *Pay-for-Play: A History of Big-Time College Athletic Reform* (Urbana: University of Illinois Press, 2011): 71–88.

121. John F. Kennedy, "Remarks to Delegates of the Youth Fitness Conference," February 21, 1961, Adobe Flash audio, John F. Kennedy Presidential Library and Museum. https://www.jfklibrary.org/Asset-Viewer/Archives/JFKWHA-012–002.aspx.

122. John F. Kennedy Presidential Library and Museum, "The Federal Government Takes On Physical Fitness." n.d. https://www.jfklibrary.org/JFK/JFK-in-History/Physical-Fitness.aspx.

123. Olympic-museum.de, "Medal Table Olympic Games 1952 Helsinki." n.d. http://olympic-museum.de/m-stand/olympic-games-medal-table-1952.php.

124. Olympic-museum.de, "Medal Table Olympic Games 1956 Stockholm." n.d. http://olympic-museum.de/m-stand/olympic-games-medal-table-1956.php.

125. Olympic-museum.de, "Medal Table Olympic Games 1960 Rome." n.d. http://olympic-museum.de/m-stand/olympic-games-medal-table-1960.php.

126. Olympic-museum.de, "Medal Table Olympic Games 1964 Tokyo." n.d. http://olympic-museum.de/m-stand/olympic-games-medal-table-1964.php.

127. The Intercollegiate Athletic Association of the United States. Proceedings of the Fourth Annual Convention Held at New York City, New York, Article VII (December 28, 1909): 68.

128. Smith, Ronald A., *Pay for Play. A History of Big-Time College Athletic Reform.* (Urbana, Chicago, Springfield: University of Illinois Press, 2011): 61.

129. Porto, Brian L. *The Supreme Court and the NCAA: The Case for Less Commercialism and More Due Process in College Sports.* (Ann Arbor: University of Michigan Press, 2012): 25.

130. Walter Byers, with Chris Hammer. *Unsportsmanlike Conduct: Exploiting College Athletes* (Ann Arbor: University of Michigan Press, 2010): 70–71.

131. Byers and Hammer, *Unsportsmanlike Conduct*, 69.

132. Leonard Koppet, "Baker Field: Birthplace of Sports Television." n.d. http://www.college.columbia.edu/cct_archive/spr99/34a.html

133. Jeffrey Montez de Oca, "A Cartel in the Public Interest: NCAA Broadcast Policy." *American Studies* 49, no. 3¾ (Fall/Winter 2008): 157–94.

134. Edward H. Clarke, *Sex in Education: A Fair Chance for Girls* (Boston: Houghton, Mifflin, 1884): 14–15.

135. Clarke, *Sex in Education*, 18.

136. Clarke, *Sex in Education*, 69.

137. Clarke, *Sex in Education*, 117.

138. Clarke, *Sex in Education*, 126–27 and 131–32.

139. Julia Ward Howe, *Sex and Education: A Reply to Dr. E.H. Clark's Sex in Education* (Boston: Robert Brothers, 1874): 180.

140. Howe, *Sex and Education*, 15.

141. Howe, *Sex and Education*, 87–88.

142. Senda Berenson (ed.), *Basket Ball for Women* (New York: American Sports, 1903): 5–13.

143. Florence A. Somers, *The Principles of Women's Athletics* (New York: Barnes, 1930): advertisement facing title page.

144. Deborah Brake and Elizabeth Caitlin, "The Path of Most Resistance: The Long Road toward Gender Equity in Intercollegiate Athletics." *Duke Journal of Gender Law & Policy* 3, no. 51 (1996): 51–92 and 52–53.

145. Michigan State University Archives and Historical Collections. U.A.12.3.8.

146. Michigan State University Archives and Historical Collections. U.A.12.3.18. and Michigan State University Department of Sports History, "Subject—Green Splash." http://sports.history.msu.edu/exhibit.php?kid=5–14-7.

147. Laura Grindstaff and Emily West, "Cheerleading and the Gendered Politics of Sport." *Social Problems* 53, no. 4 (November 2006): 500–18.

148. Pamela Grundy, "From Amazons to Glamazons: The Rise and Fall of North Carolina Women's Basketball, 1920–1960." *Journal of American History* (June 2000): 112–45.

149. Grundy, "From Amazons to Glamazons," 140.

150. US Department of Justice, "Overview of Title IX of the Education Amendments of 1972." n.d. https://www.justice.gov/crt/overview-title-ix-education-amendments-1972–20-usc-1681-et-seq.

151. US Department of Labor, "Title IX, Education Amendments of 1972." n.d. https://www.dol.gov/oasam/regs/statutes/titleix.htm.

152. Women's Sports Foundation, "Title IX Legislative Chronology." https://www.womenssportsfoundation.org/advocate/title-ix-issues/history-title-ix/history-title-ix.

153. Women's Sports Foundation, "Title IX Legislative Chronology."

154. US Department of Education. Policy Interpretation-Title IX and Intercollegiate Athletics, 45 C.F.R. Part 26 (1979); OCR's Title IX Athletics Investigators Manual (1990). https://www.justice.gov/crt/title-ix#10.%C2%A0%20Athletics%20(ï%C2%BD§%20__.450.

155. *Grove City College v. Bell*, 465 U.S. 555 (1984)1.

156. Civil Rights Restoration Act of 1987. https://www.govtrack.us/congress/bills/100/s557.

157. *Haffer v. Temple University*, 688 F. 2d 14 (1982). http://openjurist.org/688/f2d/14/haffer-v-temple-university.

158. *Franklin v. Gwinnett Co. Public Schools*, 503 U.S. 60 (1991). https://www.law.cornell.edu/supremecourt/text/503/60#writing-USSC_CR_0503_0060_ZS.

159. 1994 Equity in Athletics Disclosure Act. https://www.congress.gov/bill/103rd-congress/house-bill/921.

160. *Cohen v. Brown University*, 101 F. 3d 155 (1996). http://openjurist.org/101/f3d/155/cohen-v-brown-university.

161. Brake and Caitlin, "The Path of Most Resistance," 51–92, 61

162. Brake and Caitlin, "The Path of Most Resistance," 67.

163. Title IX Info, "Legal Cases." http://www.titleix.info/Resources/Legal-Cases.aspx.

164. Brake and Caitlin, "The Path of Most Resistance," 62.

165. OCR's Title IX Athletics Investigators Manual (1990).

166. Women's Sports Foundation, "Title IX Legislative Chronology."

167. Tyler Kingkade, "There Are Far More Title IX Investigations on Colleges than Most People Know," *Huffington Post*, June 16, 2016. http://www.huffingtonpost.com/entry/title-ix-investigations-sexual-harassment_us_575f4b0ee4b053d433061b3d; Tyler Kingkade, "List of 195 Higher Institutions Under Title IX Sexual Violence Investigations," DocumentCloud.org. https://www.documentcloud.org/documents/2861781-List-of-195-Higher-Ed-Institutions-Under-Title.html.

168. Deborah J. Anderson and John J. Cheslock, "Institutional Strategies to Achieve Gender Equity in Intercollegiate Athletics: Does Title IX Harm Male Athletes?," *American Economic Review* 94, no.2 (May 2004): 307–11; Deborah J. Anderson, John J. Cheslock, and Ronald G. Ehrenberg, "Gender Equity in Intercollegiate Athletics: Determinants of Title IX Compliance." *Journal of Higher Education* 77, no. 2 (March/April 2006): 225–50.

169. NCAA, "Women's Water Polo," n.d. http://www.ncaa.com/sports/waterpolo-women; NCAA, "Women's Ice Hockey," n.d. http://www.ncaa.com/sports/icehockey-women/nc.

170. Anderson, Cheslock, and Ehrenberg, "Gender Equity in Intercollegiate Athletics;" Anderson and Cheslock, "Institutional Strategies to achieve Gender Equity in Intercollegiate Athletics."

171. Michael Hurd, *Black College Football, 1892–1992. One Hundred Years of History, Education and Pride* (Marceline, MO: Walsworth, 2000).

172. W. Montague Cobb, "Race and Runners." *Journal of Health and Physical Education* 7, no. 1 (January 1936): 5. http://dh.howard.edu/cgi/viewcontent.cgi?article=1012&context=soci_fac.

173. Cobb, "Race and Runners," 4.

174. Elmer D. Mitchell, *Intramural Athletics* (New York: Barnes, 1925).

175. Wilbur P. Bowen and Elmer D. Mitchell, *The Theory of Organized Play: Its Nature and Significance* (New York: Barnes, 1928.)

176. Elmer D. Mitchell, "Racial Traits in Athletics." *American Physical Education Review* 27, no. 4 (April 1922): 20–21.

177. Elmer D. Mitchell, "Racial Traits in Athletics," 21.

178. Elmer D. Mitchell, "Racial Traits in Athletics," 20.

179. Mitchell, "Racial Traits in Athletics," 21.

180. Albert Gehring, *Racial Contrasts: Distinguishing the Traits of the Greco-Latins and Teutons* (New York: Putnam, 1908).

181. Booker T. Washington, "Inferior and Superior Races." *North American Review* 201: 538–42; and his chapter on "The Negro Race" at the First National Conference on Race Betterment, 410–420.

182. Daniel G. Brinton, *Races and Peoples* (New York: Hodges, 1890).

183. Joel Perlman, "Race or People: Federal Race Classifications for Europeans in America: 1898–1913" (Working Paper no. 320, Levy Institute, 2001).

184. Mitchell, "Racial Traits in Athletics," 1.

185. Mitchell, "Racial Traits in Athletics," 2.

186. Mitchell, "Racial Traits in Athletics," 12.

187. Mitchell, "Racial Traits in Athletics," 13.

188. Cobb, "Race and Runners," 5.

189. Cobb, "Race and Runners," 6.

190. Cobb, "Race and Runners," 9.

191. Charles H. Martin, "Racial Change and 'Big-Time' College Football in Georgia: The Age of Segregation, 1892–1957." *Georgia Historical Quarterly* 80, no. 3 (Fall 1996): 532–562.

192. Edward Wong, "College Football: N.Y.U. Honors Protesters It Punished in '41," *New York Times*, May 4, 2010.

193. Mike Celizic, *The Biggest Game of Them All. Notre Dame, Michigan State, and the Fall of '66* (New York and London: Simon & Schuster, 1992).

194. Steven Travers, *One Night Two Teams: Alabama vs. USC and the Game That Changed A Nation* (Lanham, MD: Taylor Trade Publishing, 2007).

195. Bobby L. Lovett, "Edward S. Temple," *Tennessee Encyclopedia of History and Culture*, February 28, 2011. http://tennesseeencyclopedia.net/entry.php?rec=1304.

196. Frank Litsky, "Wilma Rudolph, Star of the 1960 Olympics, Dies at 54," *New York Times*, November 13, 1994. http://www.nytimes.com/1994/11/13/obituaries/wilma-rudolph-star-of-the-1960-olympics-dies-at-54.html.

197. Pete Axthelm, "Boycott Now—Boycott Later?," *Sports Illustrated*, February 26, 1968. https://www.si.com/vault/1968/02/26/547303/boycott-nowboycott-later.

198. Joseph Sheehan, "Two Black Power Advocates Ousted from Olympics," *New York Times*, October 18, 1968. http://www.nytimes.com/learning/general/onthisday/big/1018.html.

199. Lane Demas, *Integrating the Gridiron: Black Civil Rights and American College Football* (New Brunswick, NJ: Rutgers University Press, 2010).

200. J.M. Smith, "Breaking the Plane: Integration and Black Protest in Michigan State University during the 1960s," *Michigan Historical Review* 33, no. 2 (Fall 2007): 101–129.

201. Bentley Historical Library, "The Michigan Stadium Story. The First 'Broadcast' of U of M Football," last updated April 15, 2007. http://bentley.umich.edu/athdept/stadium/stadtext/mattice.htm.

202. Ibid.

203. Michigan State University Department of Sports History, "Athletic Facilities." n.d. http://sports.history.msu.edu/exhibit.php?kid=5-14-0.

204. Ronald A. Smith, *Play-by-Play: Radio, Television and Big-Time College Sport* (Baltimore: Johns Hopkins University Press, 2001): 14–15.

205. Smith, *Play-by-Play,* 15.

206. Smith, *Play-by-Play,* 23–25.

207. Smith, *Play-by-Play,* 17.

208. Lou Schwartz, "Sportscasting Firsts: 1920–Present," American Sportscasters Online. n.d. http://www.americansportscastersonline.com/sportscastingfirsts .html.

209. Kathleen M. O'Toole, "Intercollegiate Football and Educational Radio: Three Case Studies of the Commercialization of Sports Broadcasting in the 1920s and 1930s" (PhD diss., Pennsylvania State University, 2010): 51–98.

210. Smith, *Play-by-Play,* 212.

211. O'Toole, "Intercollegiate Football and Educational Radio," 99–196.

212. Leonard Koppett, "Baker Field: Birthplace of Sports Television." n.d. http://www.college.columbia.edu/cct_archive/spr99/34a.html.

213. Ibid.

214. Edgerton, Gary R. *The Columbia History of American Television* (New York: Columbia University Press, 2007): 85.

215. Edgerton, *The Columbia History of American Television,* 56.

216. Eric Vander Voort, "First Televised Football Game Featured Fordham, Waynesburg in 1939," National Collegiate Athletic Association, September 29, 2015. http://www.ncaa.com/news/football/article/2014-09-28/first-televised-football-game-featured-fordham-waynesburg-1939.

217. Ibid.

218. Edgerton, *The Columbia History of American Television,* 84–86.

219. Smith, *Play-by-Play,* 55.

220. Smith, *Play-by-Play,* 57.

221. Jeffrey Montez de Oca, "A Cartel in the Public Interest: NCAA Broadcast Policy during the Early Cold War." *American Studies* 49, no. 3/4 (Fall/Winter 2008): 162.

222. Montez de Oca, "A Cartel in the Public Interest," 166–168.

223. Montez de Oca, "A Cartel in the Public Interest," 170.

224. Montez de Oca, "A Cartel in the Public Interest," 171.

225. Montez de Oca, "A Cartel in the Public Interest," 172.

226. Roone Arledge, *Roone: A Memoir* (New York: HarperCollins, 2003): 30–31.

227. Arledge, *Roone,* 31.

228. Arledge, *Roone,* 33.

229. Montez de Oca, "A Cartel in the Public Interest," 173.

230. Mike Celizic, *The Biggest Game of Them All: Notre Dame, Michigan State and the Fall of '66* (New York: Simon & Schuster, 1992).

231. Montez de Oca, "A Cartel in the Public Interest," 176.

232. Thomas Scully, "NCAA v. Board of Regents of the University of Oklahoma. NCAA's Television Plan Is Sacked by the Sherman Antitrust Act." *Catholic University Law Review* 34, no. 3 (1985): 857–887. http://scholarship.law.edu/cgi/viewcontent.cgi?article=2067&context=lawreview.

233. Rick Warner, "Bird v. Magic. Their 1979 Matchup Took Ratings to Still Unequal High," *LA Times*, April 2, 1989. http://articles.latimes.com/1989–04-02/sports/sp-1483_1_bird-magic-game.

234. Illinois High School Association, "A Brief History of March Madness." n.d. http://www.ihsa.org/SportsActivities/MarchMadnessExperience/MarchMadnessHistory.aspx.

235. David Eskenazi, "Wayback Machine: Genesis of 'March Madness.'" Sports-pressNW.com, March 25, 2014. http://sportspressnw.com/2181842/2014/wayback-machine-genesis-of-march-madness.

236. Karen Weaver, "Media Deals, College Football and Governance: Who Is in Charge?" *Change: The Magazine of Higher Learning* 45, no. 4 (2013): 15. (The 2013 ACC-Notre Dame agreement applies to all sports except football. Notre Dame's commitment, however, is to schedule four to six football games against ACC members every season, so technically, the Notre Dame football program joined the ACC but only partially).

237. NCAA.com, "Turner, CBS and the NCAA Reach Long-Term Multimedia Rights Extension for NCAA Division I Men's Basketball Championship," National Collegiate Athletic Association, April 12, 2016. http://www.ncaa.com/news/basketball-men/article/2016–04-12/turner-cbs-and-ncaa-reach-long-term-multimedia-rights.

238. NCAA.com, "Turner, CBS and the NCAA Reach Long-Term Multimedia Rights Extension for NCAA Division I Men's Basketball Championship."

239. NCAA.com, "Turner, CBS and the NCAA Reach Long-Term Multimedia Rights Extension for NCAA Division I Men's Basketball Championship."

240. Mark Ozanian, "Forbes Fab 40. The Most Valuable Sports Brands," *Forbes*, October 24, 2016. https://www.forbes.com/pictures/mlm45gelhg/7-college-basketball-fi/#4ae3d35b486d.

241. John D. Colombo, "The NCAA, Tax Exemption and College Athletics" (PhD diss., Pennsylvania State University, 2009): 10. https://pennstatelaw.psu.edu/_file/NCAA26.pdf.

242. Derek Volner, "ESPN Presents MegaCast Production for College Football Playoff National Championship Presented by AT&T—Clemson vs. Alabama," ESPN MediaZone, January 5, 2017. http://espnmediazone.com/us/press-releases/2017/01/espn-presents-megacast-production-college-football-playoff-national-championship-presented-att-clemson-vs-alabama.

243. Volner, "ESPN Presents Megacast Production College Football Playoff National Championship Presented by AT&T—Clemson v. Alabama, Espnmediazone.com."

244. Derek Volner, "More than 26 Million Viewers Watched the College Football Playoff National Championship Game." ESPN MediaZone, January 10, 2017. http://espnmediazone.com/us/press-releases/2017/01/26-million-viewers-watched-college-football-playoff-national-championship/

245. James Duderstadt, *Intercollegiate Athletics and the American University: A University President's Perspective* (Ann Arbor: University of Michigan Press, 2000): 11.

246. Robert D. "Benford, The College Sports Reform Movement: Reframing the 'Edutainment' Industry." *Sociological Quarterly* 48, no. 1 (Winter 2007): 1–28, 4.

247. Ann Scales, "Student Gladiators and Sexual Assault: A New Analysis of Liabilities for Injuries Inflicted by College Athletes." *Michigan Gender & Law* 205 (2009): 205–285.

248. Scales, "Student Gladiators and Sexual Assault."

249. Jason Slotkin, "Ex-Penn State President Guilty of Child Endangerment in Abuse Scandal." *Two Way*, NPR, March 24, 2017. http://www.npr.org/sections/thetwo-way/2017/03/24/521427407/ex-penn-state-president-guilty-of-child-endangerment-in-abuse-scandal.

250. Evans, Tim, Alesia, Mark, and Kwiatkowski, Marisa. "Former USA Gymnastics Doctor Accused of Sexual Abuse." *Indianapolis Star.* September 12, 2016. https://www.indystar.com/story/news/2016/09/12/former-usa-gymnastics-doctor-accused-abuse/89995734/

251. Geraci, Carly. "Editorial: Simon, Enablers, Need to Resign." *State News.* January 19, 2018. http://statenews.com/article/2018/01/editorial-simon-enablers-need-to-resign-so-survivors-can-move-on

252. Branch Taylor, "The Shame of College Sports," *Atlantic*, October 2011.

253. Walter Byers with Charles Hammer, *Unsportsmanlike Conduct: Exploiting College Athletes* (Ann Arbor: University of Michigan Press, 2010).

254. Duderstadt, *Intercollegiate Athletics and the American University.*

255. Andrew Zimbalist, *Unpaid Professionals: Commercialism and Conflict in Big-Time College Sports* (Princeton, NJ: Princeton University Press, 1999).

256. Murray Sperber, *Beer and Circus: How Big-Time College Sports Are Crippling Undergraduate Education* (New York: Holt, 2000).

257. Ronald A. Smith, *Pay for Play: A History of Big-Time College Athletic Reform* (Urbana: University of Illinois Press, 2013).

258. Knight Commission on Intercollegiate Athletics. Home page. n.d. http://www.knightcommission.org.

259. Drake Group, "Drake Group Establishes "In Residence" Status at the University of New Haven." n.d. https://thedrakegroup.org/2013/01/14/drake-group-helps-to-pass-athletes-right-to-know-act.

260. Nate Silver, "Expansion by Big Ten May Bring Small Payoff," *FiveThirtyEight*, November 20, 2012. https://fivethirtyeight.com/features/expansion-by-big-ten-may-bring-small-payoff.

261. s.2727 Amateur Sports Act, Congress.gov, November 11, 1978. https://www.congress.gov/bill/95th-congress/senate-bill/2727.

CPSIA information can be obtained
at www.ICGtesting.com
Printed in the USA
LVHW020712110723
752054LV00008B/25